# The Legal Writing
# Survival Guide

# The Legal Writing
# Survival Guide

Rachel H. Smith

CAROLINA ACADEMIC PRESS
Durham, North Carolina

Library of Congress Cataloging-in-Publication Data

Smith, Rachel H.
The legal writing survival guide / Rachel H. Smith.
    p. cm.
Includes index.
ISBN 978-1-61163-145-6 (alk. paper)
1. Legal composition--United States. 2. Law--United States--Language. 3. Report writing--United States. I. Title.

KF250.S625 2012
808.06'634--dc23

                    2012015404


CAROLINA ACADEMIC PRESS
700 Kent Street
Durham, North Carolina 27701
Telephone (919) 489-7486
Fax (919) 493-5668
www.cap-press.com

Printed in the United States of America

*For Lipkin, Oscar, and Gus*

# Contents

# Acknowledgments

I am so grateful to my colleagues and friends who read the manuscript and provided helpful feedback: Jill Barton, Alyssa Dragnich, Amy Rodriguez, Rosi Schrier, and David Switzer. In addition, thank you to all of my LComm colleagues for your encouragement. And thank you to Dean Patricia White and the University of Miami School of Law for supporting this book.

I am also grateful to my former colleagues at Santa Clara University School of Law and Quinn Emanuel Urquhart & Sullivan, LLP for teaching me so much about legal writing.

I am grateful to Julie Showers and David Deide for the graphics.

And I am grateful for my family. Thank you to Daniel Lipkin for being a great editor and for cracking me up. Thank you to Oscar the Cat and Gus the Cat for writing this book with me. Thank you to Shaina Feinberg for being a source of light. And thank you to my parents, Leah Rose Abrams and Gary L. Smith. I am lucky to have parents who love books and can answer grammar questions at any time of the day or night.

Last, I am grateful to my former and current students. You have inspired, tormented (you know who you are), amused, and delighted me. I wrote this book for you.

# Introduction:
# The Will to Survive

This book is about survival. Being a lawyer is hard. Doing the work of a lawyer is hard. Reading rules, analyzing facts, solving problems, and writing in a way that another person can understand is hard. I had days as a law student and a lawyer that I would swear were harder to survive than being lost in the Everglades, marooned in Antarctica, or adrift in the Indian Ocean. This book offers advice, processes, tips, and tactics to help you survive any legal writing project. They are all born of my real-life experience as a litigator at a large firm and as a legal writing professor.

Before we get any further, you should know that this book, like any survival guide, makes one fundamental assumption about its reader: that he or she *wants* to survive. Just by picking up this book, you have demonstrated the will to survive. You are not going to be the person who lies down in the snow on Mount Everest and tells the rest of the survivors to go on without you. You know the one: "I am so cold. I can't go on. Leave me here. Oh, I see my Nana coming towards me. She is so beautiful...."

It may seem over the top to talk about "survival" in the context of writing legal documents. Obviously, there are people who actually worry every day about how to survive. Law students and lawyers occupy a place of comfort compared to so many others (even if that is easy to forget). And yes, we are deeply grateful for that good fortune. But in my experience, there were memos, motions, emails, and a million other documents that felt like a matter of life or death while I was writing them. I wrote this book with the hope that I could help you have more perspective in those moments than I did.

I also wrote this book because I think that you can be a good legal writer, and that the writing that we do as lawyers is worthwhile. Being able to write in a way that communicates effectively and helps your client is a tremendous thing—and it *feels* tremendous to do it well, like having a super power. I imagine that surviving a zombie apocalypse or a rhinoceros attack feels the same way. I want you to have that feeling when you survive writing a legal document.

This book is for law students and lawyers who are in the midst of a struggle to survive with a legal document. If that describes you, I think that this book will help you and make your life easier. But here is my first tip: Even if you follow none of the steps in this book, even if you read this book (or don't) and then do the opposite of everything I suggest, you will still survive as long as you have a friend, or a cat, or a couch to go home to. Because that is how you really survive the stresses of this profession—by not neglecting your life away from your work computer. The way to survive is to remember the people, places, animals, books, and things you love. And keep your feet dry.

I wish the best for you in all of your adventures, legal writing and otherwise. Godspeed!

# The Legal Writing
# Survival Guide

# Chapter I

# Surviving Legal Writing

You have a legal writing assignment. And it is not going well. I get it. Trust me. I have been there. But now you have this book to help you. Find the section that discusses the problem (or problems) you are having. Then, start fixing them.

## A. How to Start Any Document[1]

Starting is often the hardest part. Getting started means jumping into the icy water with the sharks and polar bears and who knows what else. But how can you start if what you are writing has to be perfect and every wasted minute takes it further and further from that vision of legal writing perfection that you know everyone is expecting? How can you start if you are not going to have enough time to do the best possible job? How can you start if you just realized that you need to clean your entire office and water all of your sad, sickly plants, like that one over there that you got when you were hopeful and happy and did not have this terrible assignment hanging over you?

You can start because you have to start. Here is the truth: This assignment is not going away. It is like a bill that comes in the mail. You do not get out of paying it by not opening the envelope. (I have tried. They send more bills!) So the longer you put off what-

---

1. This chapter assumes you have already completed the research for your document. If you have not, that is OK. Check out Chapter V, Section A.

ever this epic writing assignment happens to be, the less time you give yourself to actually do a good job.

Here are five steps to help you start writing and stop suffering: 1) focus on done-ness, not perfection, 2) adopt the psychology of survival through perspective and optimism, 3) make a plan for your document, 4) start with something simple, and 5) bite the bullet and write some topic sentences.

## 1. Focus on Done-Ness, Not Perfection

Your vision of legal writing perfection is an illusion. The key to starting any document is to forget about how perfect you think it has to be. Perfectionism is usually the underlying reason for procrastination. Especially among us high-achieving types, perfectionism is the man hiding behind the curtain, pulling the levers of procrastination.

You are afraid to start writing because you do not want to write something that is not perfect. I know this feeling well. Here is the proof: I wrote that last sentence fifteen times. But your perfectionism is not doing you any favors right now. Why? Because at the beginning of the writing process, perfectionism stops you from doing the one thing you need to do—which is to start writing the dumb document.

Listen. Your document is not going to be "perfect" no matter what you do. Does the idea of writing something less than perfect cause you to feel a deep pain in the center of your soul? If so, you are a perfectionist and you need to come back to planet Earth. Pronto. Here is a rule that applies to tents as well as legal documents: a pretty good one is better than none at all.

You have to change your mindset from one that is concerned with perfection to one that is concerned with survival. When you cannot get started, survival boils down to done-ness. I do not mean done-ness like a turkey. I mean done-ness like, "I am finally done writing this document." Done-ness is your new goal. A document cannot be good, effective, helpful, or well written until it is done. An unfinished document, even one written with the loftiest, most perfectionistic intentions, does not do anyone any good. Lawyers write in the real world. And in the real world, your document has to be done.

And if you think about it for a second, what is a perfect legal document anyway? If perfect means that your boss or professor will not have any comments, you can forget it. In the time that I have been a lawyer and a legal writing professor, I have never written a document that was returned to me without any suggestions about how to improve it, nor have I reviewed a document that was so ideal in every way that I could not offer a single suggestion of my own. Legal writing is not like arithmetic. There is not just one right answer. So anyone who reads your document is probably going to have some comment about how to make it better. Trying to write something so perfect that the reviewing attorney would not dream of altering even a single syllable is like looking for an ice cream parlor in the arid nothingness of the Gobi Desert.

If you never received critical feedback, you would never learn anything. There is absolutely nothing wrong with learning something. You should look at feedback as a learning opportunity, not a judgment on your ultimate value as a human being. I know that this can be really hard. I take everything very personally. When I would receive a document covered in comments and corrections, I would want to throw myself out my office window. But if I had let my oversensitivity blind me to the useful feedback that I was receiving, I would be the same writer today that I was when I graduated from high school. And that writer thought it was appropriate to dot her i's with smiley faces.

Rather than dreading the feedback that makes you feel like your document is not perfect, you should welcome it. And in those rare instances where you turn in a document and the reviewing attorney has nothing to say, you should be concerned. Because that means he or she likely did not read it closely, which means the document could be riddled with any number of mistakes that you, and you alone, must catch.

Right now, you need to start writing this document. Put your perfectionism aside so you can write *something*. Do not worry. You are not going to turn in a pile of gibberish. We will work on making this document as good as possible later, after we have something to work with. It is easier to turn something OK into something awesome, than to create something awesome out of a blank screen and a puddle of tears.

## 2. Adopt the Psychology of Survival

Once you have cured your perfectionism, you need to replace it with something more helpful, like positive thinking. Positive thinking sometimes gets mocked for being silly or naïve. But having an optimistic outlook is a key to survival. Being able to conjure a positive attitude will make the process of writing this document a million times more bearable. The document must get written. But you can choose to write this document with a heart full of cynicism and loathing or with the spirit of hopefulness and good cheer. Why make the experience worse than it has to be? You have to spend all your time with your attitude, so having a bad one is like being stuck in a lifeboat with a jerk. Except that this jerk lives inside your brain! Throw the jerk overboard, and start thinking positively.

To cultivate a positive outlook you need two things: perspective and optimism.

First, perspective helps you remember that this document is not the most important thing in the world. Nor will it be the worst thing anyone has ever had to endure. It is just a document. And you just have to write it. In the scheme of things, the stakes are very low. Imagine the situations that people have survived—shark attacks, plane crashes in the Arctic, trips to the dentist. You can totally do this. If you can start thinking that this document is not such a big deal, it will help you get started. Adopting this more reasonable perspective does not mean that you are going to do a bad job or not try your best. It just means that your life does not depend on writing this document.[2]

---

2. Even if someone's life *does* depend on you writing this document, it is probably better to put that out of your mind as you try to get started. You will certainly want to think about that at some point in the writing process, but if you can lower the pressure at the outset, it will help you get started sooner, which will result in a better document later.

Second, optimism allows you to expect a good outcome for any writing project. Optimism means believing that everything is working out for you. When you are optimistic, you know that this document is going to come together and result in a good outcome. Tell yourself that this document is going to be great, and pretty soon, you will start to believe it.

I suggest writing some affirmations on sticky notes and taping them to your computer screen. I have these two affirmations on my computer right this second: "This document is not such a big deal." "This document is going to turn out great." Feel free to personalize your affirmations to say anything that resonates with you. You just want to have something positive in your line of sight. As you write your document, your affirmations will remind you to have a positive outlook.

## 3. Make a Plan for Your Document

Letting go of perfectionism and adopting a positive attitude puts you in a great place to start your document. The next step is to make a plan. You would not go into the wilderness without a map, so do not start working on a document without a plan. This five-step pre-writing plan will help you orient yourself in the woods, find a trail to safety, and get home in time for supper.

The five steps of the pre-writing plan are 1) verify the purpose of your document, 2) set a deadline, 3) determine a page or word limit, 4) collect all supporting documents, and 5) find a good template.

### a. Verify Your Purpose

First, make sure you have a good idea of what you are supposed to be writing about. A *really* good idea. You should be able to describe the purpose of the document in one clear and concise sentence. If you cannot — and you would not be the first — review Chapter I, Section D for help. There is no point getting started if you do not know what you are starting or why.

## b. Set a Deadline

Second, set the date and time by which you will finish this thing. This could be the date it is due. But it would be better to build in a cushion, so that you have time before it is due to review it with fresh eyes and do some more proofreading. If you have the luxury, set this deadline two days before it is due. Or two hours, if you are really up against the wall. Or two minutes, if you are anything like most of the law students and lawyers I know.

## c. Determine a Page or Word Limit

Third, make sure you know how long the document can or should be. Knowing the outer page or word limit can be comforting because it makes the document more concrete and less abstract and terrifying. If this is a document that you are submitting to a court, check the local rules to confirm the page or word limit. If this is an internal memo or a piece of correspondence, look at relevant examples to estimate an appropriate limit.

## d. Collect All Supporting Documents

Fourth, collect all the relevant documents that you need. You can put them in a physical or electronic folder. This folder should have all of the relevant instructions, rules, factual documents, pleadings, cases, and statutes. You have now defined the limited universe of sources for this particular document.

If you are a procrastinator, you should be careful with this step. You cannot allow the collection of relevant documents to become another opportunity to delay getting started. You do not want to step into the deep quicksand of document collection. Getting these documents together is just a means to an end. Once you have collected the major documents you should move on.

## e. Find a Good Template

Last, you need to start with a good template and avoid facing the scary whiteness of an empty screen. If you are writing a memo, you can use one of your earlier memos. If you are writing a brief, you can use an earlier brief in the same case, or a similar brief in a different case. If you do not know where to find a good template, ask your supervising attorney. By getting your supervising attorney to identify a useful template, you will not only have a good place to start, you will also have a better idea of what that attorney is expecting.

Using a template is a great way to get started. Templates, however, come with two huge caveats. First, you should not keep anything from the template that is not appropriate for the new document. You have to check any holdovers to make sure they belong. For example, make sure you change the date and the caption. And do not import the legal standard from your old document into the new one, unless it somehow also applies to your new document. Second, you have to validate everything you keep from the template. For example, you have to double check the format against the current local rules, make sure any research is up to date, and confirm any citations.

Smart lawyers use templates. But dopey lawyers use templates too. The dopey lawyers just do so sloppily.

## 4. Start with Something Simple

Now that you know the deadline, the length, the universe of supporting documents, and the purpose of your document, you should start thinking substantively. As you have probably anticipated, a good way to start your document is by making an outline. Understandably, by the time you finish your first semester of law school, the concept of "outlining" can be fraught with emotional baggage. Any super strict ideas about what outlining means, or what it has to involve, will only make the prospect of outlining a document that already has you tied up in knots even more unappealing.

So I am not going to make you completely outline your document. I swear. Traditional outlining may not be for you. Like chunky peanut butter, it is not to everyone's taste. But even if you are firmly anti-outline, you can still do some planning. And if you do not want to call it an outline, that is fine with me. Call it anything you want.

The three steps to starting with something simple are 1) create the shell, 2) brainstorm a substantive checklist, and 3) write anything.

## a. Create the Shell

Start by putting your document in the correct font, in the right size, with proper margins, and with page numbers. Do this even (or especially) if you are using a template. If you do not know the proper format for your document, check the instructions or the local rules. Right now. Go!

Next, lay out all of the sections of your document. A memo usually has the following components:

1) heading,
2) question presented,
3) short answer,
4) statement of facts,
5) discussion, and
6) conclusion.

Similarly, a brief usually has the following components:

1) caption,
2) introduction,
3) statement of facts,
4) argument, and
5) conclusion.[3]

Insert the heading for each section. If you are using a template, delete any parts that are not appropriate for your document and make sure everything is in the right place. If you are preparing an email or a letter, put in the necessary formalities, attach any attachments, and get the basic document set up.

---

3. Now obviously these may vary based on style, preference, and local practice. For example, in many jurisdictions, you need to have a "notice" before the brief in support of a motion. Those kinds of procedural documents are super easy to whip up from a template. So definitely do them first. That can be a less stressful way to get started on your document.

Now you have a shell to work with. Soon, like a little hermit crab, the substance of your document will move into the shell, and life will be wonderful.

### b. Brainstorm a Substantive Checklist

Next, identify the main points you need to discuss in your document. If you are writing a memo, the main point is the legal conclusion you are explaining to your client or a senior attorney. If you are writing a motion, the main point is the conclusion you want the court to reach. If you are writing an email or letter, the main point is the most important piece of information you have to convey to the recipient. Do not forget that your document may have more than one main point.

Often, it is easier to think of questions than answers. So you will build the substance of your document through a series of questions. Start this process by writing each main point in the form of a question. You can type these questions right into the body of your document where your analysis will ultimately live.

For example, say you were writing a memo on behalf of a defendant to analyze whether the plaintiff in a breach of contract case had blown the statute of limitations. You could start by writing the following:

> Did Plaintiff file her case after the expiration of the statute of limitations?

Once you have written your main point(s) as questions, list under each main point the series of questions you have to answer to get to your main point. Your breach of contract example would look like this:

> Did Plaintiff file her case after the expiration of the statute of limitations?
>
> 1. What is Plaintiff's claim?
> 2. What is the statute of limitations for Plaintiff's claim?
> 3. When did the statute of limitations start to run?
> 4. When did the statute of limitations expire?

5.  When did Plaintiff file her claim for breach of contract?
6.  Does Plaintiff have any excuse for her late filing?
7.  Will that excuse succeed? Why or why not?
8.  What is the legal impact of the late filing?

Next, write the answers to these questions as sentences or paragraphs. Include complete citations to the authorities that support your answers.

Did Plaintiff file her case after the expiration of the statute of limitations?

1.  What is Plaintiff's claim? *Plaintiff's claim is for breach of a written contract.*
2.  What is the statute of limitations for Plaintiff's claim? *The statute of limitations for breach of a written contract is four years. Statute § 100.*[4]
3.  When did the statute of limitations start? *The statute of limitations began to run on June 28, 2007, when the breach occurred. See Smith v. Smith, 100 F. 100, 101 (13th Cir. 1901) (holding that the statute of limitations for breach of contract began to run at the time of breach).*
4.  When did the statute of limitations expire? *The statute of limitations expired on June 28, 2011.*
5.  When did Plaintiff file her claim for breach of contract? *Plaintiff filed her complaint on June 30, 2011.*
6.  Does Plaintiff have any excuse for her late filing? *Plaintiff argues that her filing was timely because she was not notified of the breach until June 30, 2007.*
7.  Will that excuse succeed? Why or why not? *Probably not. The facts indicate that Plaintiff knew of the breach on the day that it happened. Although she did not receive written notice of the breach until June 30, 2007, the statute of limitations is measured from the day a*

---

4. The law in this example is made up. Do not, under any circumstances, try to find the Thirteenth Circuit or rely on this book for substantive law.

*plaintiff has actual knowledge. See Jones v. Jones, 200
F. 200, 201 (14th Cir. 1902) (holding that the statute
of limitations began to run from the date of the plaintiff's knowledge of the facts of the breach, not the date
the plaintiff was officially informed of the breach).*

8.  What is the legal impact of the late filing? *Defendant
should move to dismiss the complaint. See Lee v. Lee,
300 F. 300, 301 (15th Cir. 1903) (holding that a court
can dismiss a late-filed complaint).*

Once you have answered each of your checklist questions, go
back to the main question that started your analysis. You should
now have an answer, so write that in.

Did Plaintiff file her case after the expiration of the
statute of limitations? *Yes.*

Look at that! You have a checklist of the substance of your document. You have identified the rules and facts that will comprise the
substance of the legal document that you have been asked to prepare. You are well on your way to writing this document.

## c. Write Anything

Now that you have the substance of your document, you need
to turn it into the document you have been asked to write. When
you are feeling stuck, the best place to start is with something easy.
The easy parts of the document are the low-hanging fruit that help
you survive when you first wash up on a desert island.

### i. The Facts

Almost any legal document requires a recitation of the relevant
facts. Usually, the facts are pretty easy to write. They should be especially easy because you will have identified the most important
facts in your substantive checklist. Sure, the facts can be tedious, but
that means they are a good thing to get out of the way early in the
writing process when you have more energy. And although you
might have to go back and revise them later, revising is good for you.

You really should go back and revise your fact section (as well as the rest of your document) numerous times before it goes out the door. The only danger in starting with the facts is that writing the facts can become a black hole for procrastinators. If you often find yourself getting lost in the statement of facts, this might not be where you want to begin. Instead, start with something else and do the facts near the end of your writing process.

### ii. The Conclusion

The conclusion is the easiest part of any legal document. Generally, the conclusion is just one simple sentence. So write that too. Now you have finished the facts and the conclusion. Woot!

### iii. CRAC

Now you are into the meat of your document. The best thing to do here is to go back to first principles. How is any legal analysis organized? CRAC.[5] That's right. CRAC: Conclusion-Rule-Analysis-Conclusion. You live and die by CRAC in a legal document.

So put your conclusion first. Think back to the example of the memo about the statute of limitations in a breach of contract case. Look at your checklist. What have you figured out? Write out the conclusion.

> Plaintiff filed her case after expiration of the statute of limitations.

Next, work on the rules. The rules are often the easiest part of the substantive analysis. You can start the rule section by copying and pasting[6] relevant language (with quotation marks) from the statutes and cases and adding citations. You have probably listed

---

5. You may have learned the CRAC format as IRAC, CREAC, CREXAC, TREAT, or any other of a million acronyms. What matters is that you start and finish your analysis with a conclusion, and in the middle, you explain the rules before you apply them. No mystery here.

6. This should go without saying, but you should never copy and paste out of a source that is not a primary legal authority. For example, you ab-

most of the relevant rules in your brainstorming checklist, so just copy or move them into the rule section of your CRAC. Do not worry about putting the rules in the correct order at first. It is usually easier to collect the rules and then organize them. Once you have all the rules together in one place, think about how to put them in a logical order—usually from general to specific. Take the broadest rule statement and put it first. Then, put the second broadest rule statement and put it next. Continue to follow with one rule statement after another, narrowing the rule as you go. If you have written a substantive checklist, your rules may already be organized in a logical order.

Here are the rules from the statute of limitations example:

> The statute of limitations for breach of a written contract is four years. Statute § 100. The statute of limitations begins to run "on the date that the breach occurred." *Smith v. Smith*, 100 F. 100, 101 (13th Cir. 1901) (holding that the statute of limitations for breach of contract began at the time of breach). When a plaintiff has actual knowledge of a breach, the statute of limitations runs, even if the plaintiff is "officially informed" of the breach at a later date. *See Jones v. Jones*, 200 F. 200, 201 (14th Cir. 1902) (holding that the statute of limitations began to run from the date of the plaintiff's knowledge of the facts of the breach, not the date that the plaintiff was officially informed of the breach). A court may dismiss a complaint that is filed after the statute of limitations has expired. *Lee v. Lee*, 300 F. 300, 301 (15th Cir. 1903) (dismissing a late-filed complaint).

Your rule section should now be developed. This is a good time to read your cases again. Confirm that you covered every relevant aspect of the rules discussed in the cases and that you used all of the relevant language from the cases in your document. Then, to

---

solutely cannot cut and paste from the headnotes of a case. Also, it is critical that you keep track of the source of each quotation so that your citations will be accurate.

make sure that your rule section is complete, answer the following questions:

- Are there any logical gaps in the rules you describe?
- Are there places where it would be better to paraphrase, rather than quote, the rules because the language used by the court is either unwieldy or unnecessary?
- Are there quotations that should be moved into parentheticals because they merely restate rules that you have already included?
- Is there a case that is so legally and factually similar to your case that it deserves a longer discussion?
- Is every sentence of your rule section followed by a citation?

What if you cannot do these steps because you do not know or understand the rules that you need to use in your document? This explains why you are having a hard time getting started. If you do not understand the rules, your document will never make sense to you, and the rules will never be clear to your reader.

If you are struggling with the rules, you should go back and review your research to get a better idea of what is going on. Try reading a secondary source. Or look at the case annotations after your statute. Or use the headnotes in your cases to track down the clearest statement of the rule. You have to figure the rules out *now*. Otherwise, this document is going to torture you until you do.

## 5. Bite the Bullet

Now it is time to really write this thing. The easiest way to crack the analysis section of your CRAC is to start with topic sentences. Yep. The very same topic sentences that you learned about in sixth grade. A topic sentence starts a paragraph and tells the reader your conclusion on the topic that will be discussed in that paragraph.[7]

---

7. A thesis sentence is just a topic sentence for the whole document. Your thesis sentence tells the reader your broad conclusion, while your topic

For each of the points that you will make in the analysis, write a strong topic sentence that states your conclusion. Put those topic sentences in a logical order. If you look back to your checklist, you will see that you have already identified the points you are going to make in your analysis section.

For example, the topic sentences for the statute of limitations example would look like this:

- Plaintiff filed her complaint for breach of a written contract on June 30, 2011, two days after the statute of limitations expired.
- Defendant should move to dismiss the untimely complaint.
- Plaintiff's argument that the statute of limitations did not begin to run until the date she received official notice of the breach will not succeed.

All you need to do now is write a paragraph after each of the topic sentences that proves why the topic sentence is true. You do that by applying the rules to your facts and analogizing and distinguishing the relevant facts of your case to the facts of the cases you found when doing your research. Harvesting the answers to the questions in your checklist will help you do this.

Here is what the analysis would look like for the statute of limitations example:

> Plaintiff filed her complaint for breach of a written contract on June 30, 2011, two days after the statute of limitations expired. The four-year statute of limitations on Plaintiff's claim began to run on June 28, 2007, the date the breach occurred. *See Smith*, 100 F. at 101. Plaintiff's own testimony and correspondence establishes that Plaintiff was aware of the breach on the day it happened. Similarly, in *Smith v. Smith*, the court measured the statute of limitations from the date of the breach

---

sentences serve as mini-thesis sentences for each of the points that add up to your overall conclusion.

because the plaintiff sent a letter on the day of the breach acknowledging that a breach occurred. *Id.* Defendant should move to dismiss the untimely complaint. Because Plaintiff's complaint was filed after the statute of limitations expired, Defendant will likely succeed in dismissing the complaint. *See Lee,* 300 F. at 301. In *Lee v. Lee,* the court dismissed a complaint that had been filed two days after the statute of limitations expired—just like the complaint in this case. *See id.*

Plaintiff's argument that the statute of limitations did not begin to run until the date she received official notice of the breach will not succeed. Although Plaintiff did not receive "official" written notice of the breach from Defendant until June 30, 2007, the statute of limitations is measured from the day Plaintiff had actual knowledge. *See Jones,* 200 F. at 201. Like the plaintiff in *Jones v. Jones,* Plaintiff had actual knowledge of the breach on the day it happened, so the court will measure the statute of limitations from that day, not the date of written notice. *See id.*

If you follow these steps, before you know it you will not only have started your document, but finished it too.

## B. How to Simplify a Document That Is Too Complicated

You started writing your document. For a little while, you were really on a roll. But then your document started spiraling out of control. Now you have research that points in a thousand different directions and so many sub-sub-sub-sections that you cannot think straight. Do not despair. Legal documents get complicated. Sometimes there are just too many facts, too many arguments, and too many cases, and they pile up on top of each other and make the whole thing a mess.

If your document is overly complicated, use these four steps to get it back on track: 1) remember your purpose by revisiting your thesis, 2) assess your position with a reverse outline, 3) take no prisoners by removing anything from your document that is not directly relevant to your conclusion, and 4) build a bunker of comments, questions, and footnotes.

## 1. Remember Your Purpose

Writing a complex legal document can feel like being lost at sea. You may find yourself drifting around, unsure of where to go or how to get there. When this happens, the first thing to do is remind yourself of why you are writing this document in the first place.

You can find your document's purpose by returning to your issue presented or your thesis sentence. If you do not have either of those yet, then try and write them. Doing so will clarify for you what this document is supposed to be about.

As discussed in the previous section, questions can be easier to write than answers. Writing the issue presented will help you determine your thesis because your thesis is basically the answer to your issue presented. For example, imagine a memo analyzing whether a defendant's claim is a compulsory cross-claim. In this imaginary case, the plaintiff brought a claim for breach of contract and the defendant wants to bring a claim for breach of fiduciary duty. To figure out your thesis, write a simplified issue presented by using the word "whether," like this:

> **Issue Presented**: Whether Defendant's claim for breach of fiduciary duty is a compulsory cross-claim to Plaintiff's claim for breach of contract.

After writing the issue presented, it is easy to see what the thesis sentence should be.

> **Thesis**: Defendant's claim for breach of fiduciary duty *is/is not* a compulsory cross-claim to Plaintiff's claim for breach of contract.

The thesis sentence answers the question posed in the issue presented. In this example, you just have to decide whether the breach of fiduciary duty claim is or is not a compulsory cross-claim. Because every document needs a thesis sentence, this is a useful process even if you are writing a legal document that does not require an issue presented.

## 2. Assess Your Position

Now that you know the purpose of your document, you need to determine where you are and where you need to go. One of the best ways to assess your position is to create a reverse outline. It is called a reverse outline because you write it after you have written your document, rather than beforehand like a typical outline. Creating a reverse outline is a way to retrace your steps.

The guideposts for this reverse outline should be your point headings and your topic sentences. Pull out every point heading and topic sentence and put them in order in a separate document. Now you can get a good look at them.

But wait, what are you saying? "I cannot do this exercise because my paragraphs do not have topic sentences?" Hmmm. I am starting to understand why your document is too complicated—you have rejected the major organizing principle of good writing. Your topic sentences guide you and your reader. You must write them. Topic sentences are not optional. Make friends with them, and fast. You can do this by making the first sentence of every paragraph a clear topic sentence that states the argument you are making in that paragraph.

Creating this list of your point headings and topic sentences is a quick way to understand the development of your argument. The headings and sentences should flow logically from one to the next as your argument develops. By looking at them separately, you should be able to see any gaps in your argument or places where it goes off track.

For example, here is a list of topic sentences for the paragraphs in our draft memo analyzing whether a defendant's claim for breach of fiduciary duty is a compulsory cross-claim to the plaintiff's claim for breach of contract:

1. A cross-claim is compulsory under Federal Rule of Civil Procedure 13(a)(1)(A) if it "arises out of the transaction or occurrence that is the subject matter of the opposing party's claim."[8]

2. One exception to the rule that makes any claim arising out of the same transaction or occurrence compulsory is when the claim is the subject of another pending action. Fed. R. Civ. P. 13(a)(2)(A).

3. Here, the claim for breach of fiduciary duty is compulsory because it arises out of the same contract that is the basis for Plaintiff's breach of contract claim.

4. The exception in Rule 13(a)(2)(A) does not apply because these parties are not involved in any other pending action.

5. The exception in Rule 13(a)(2)(A) applies even to claims brought in state court.

6. In *Smith v. Smith*, the court held that the exception in Rule 13(a)(2)(A) applied because the defendant had already brought suit against the plaintiff on the claim in state court.

Next, label which CRAC component each sentence or heading represents. By doing this, you can start to see where things got squirrely.

1. A cross-claim is compulsory under Federal Rule of Civil Procedure 13(a)(1)(A) if it "arises out of the transaction or occurrence that is the subject matter of the opposing party's claim." (**RULE**)

2. One exception to the rule that makes any claim arising out of the same transaction or occurrence com-

---

8. Again, these are hypothetical examples. Please do not rely on this book for substantive law.

pulsory is when the claim is the subject of another pending action. Fed. R. Civ. P. 13(a)(2)(A). (**RULE**)

3. Here, the claim for breach of fiduciary duty is compulsory because it arises out of the same contract that is the basis for Plaintiff's breach of contract claim. (**ANALYSIS**)

4. The exception in Rule 13(a)(2)(A) does not apply because these parties are not involved in any other pending action. (**ANALYSIS**)

5. The exception in Rule 13(a)(2)(A) applies even to claims brought in state court. (**RULE**)

6. In *Smith v. Smith*, the court held that the exception in Rule 13(a)(2)(A) applied because the defendant had already brought suit against the plaintiff on the claim in state court. (**RULE**)

Does anything jump out at you? How about the fact that the memo started with a rule, instead of a conclusion? And where is the final conclusion? And why do those rules in points 5 and 6 come after the analysis?

This list demonstrates one of the most common ways that a document becomes too complicated: it departs from the CRAC format. Forsaking the CRAC format in this way almost guarantees that your document will be too complicated. Your reader expects the logical CRAC format. When you do not follow it, you risk alienating and confusing your reader, which is the last thing you want to do.[9]

To fix your document's non-CRAC format you should 1) add a conclusion to the beginning, 2) put all of the rules together before the analysis, and 3) add a conclusion at the end.

1. Defendant's claim for breach of fiduciary duty is a compulsory cross-claim to Plaintiff's claim for breach of contract. (**CONCLUSION**)

---

9. Personally, the last thing that I want to do is anything that involves being in the same room with a snake, but confusing the reader is a very close second to last.

2. A cross-claim is compulsory under Federal Rule of Civil Procedure 13(a)(1)(A) if it "arises out of the transaction or occurrence that is the subject matter of the opposing party's claim." (RULE)

3. One exception to the rule that makes any claim arising out of the same transaction or occurrence compulsory is when the claim is the subject of another pending action. Fed. R. Civ. P. 13(a)(2)(A). (RULE)

4. The exception in Rule 13(a)(2)(A) applies even to claims brought in state court. (RULE)

5. In *Smith v. Smith*, the court held that the exception in Rule 13(a)(2)(A) applied because the defendant had already brought suit against the plaintiff on the claim in state court. (RULE)

6. Here, the claim for breach of fiduciary duty is compulsory because it arises out of the same contract that is the basis for Plaintiff's breach of contract claim. (ANALYSIS)

7. The exception in Rule 13(a)(2)(A) does not apply because these parties are not involved in any other pending action. (ANALYSIS)

8. Thus, Defendant's claim is a compulsory cross-claim. (CONCLUSION)

Now this memo followes the CRAC format.

## 3. Take No Prisoners

Once you have reverse outlined and labeled the CRAC components, you need to make sure that everything you wrote belongs in the document. In addition to departing from the CRAC format, most legal documents get too complicated because they do not stay focused on the relevant issues. Because honesty is important in survival situations, I am going to level with you: taking no prisoners is often the hardest part of de-complicating a document.

You have to audition every piece of information in your document. Only the essential pieces can remain. This step is like packing your backpack; you cannot include anything that you do not need to survive. Your teddy bear and Beatles records are not going to make the cut. This is not the time to be sentimental about what you have written. You might have points in your document that are clever, or interesting, or you think are written in a particularly lovely way. But if they do not directly serve the purpose of your document, you must let them go.

There should be nothing in your document that is not directly relevant to the conclusion you have reached about your case. You have to look hard at the list and try to spot tangents and digressions that take your analysis off track. Look at the compulsory cross-claim list again with an eye toward identifying tangents or digressions:

1. Defendant's claim for breach of fiduciary duty is a compulsory cross-claim to Plaintiff's claim for breach of contract. **(CONCLUSION)**

2. A cross-claim is compulsory under Federal Rule of Civil Procedure 13(a)(1)(A) if it "arises out of the transaction or occurrence that is the subject matter of the opposing party's claim." **(RULE)**

3. One exception to the rule that makes any claim arising out of the same transaction or occurrence compulsory is when the claim is the subject of another pending action. Fed. R. Civ. P. 13(a)(2)(A). **(RULE)**

4. The exception in Rule 13(a)(2)(A) applies even to claims brought in state court. **(RULE)**

5. In *Smith v. Smith*, the court held that the exception in Rule 13(a)(2)(A) applied because the defendant had already brought suit against the plaintiff on the claim in state court. **(RULE)**

6. Here, the claim for breach of fiduciary duty is compulsory because it arises out of the same contract that is the basis for Plaintiff's breach of contract claim. **(ANALYSIS)**

7. The exception in Rule 13(a)(2)(A) does not apply because these parties are not involved in any other pending action. **(ANALYSIS)**

8. Thus, Defendant's claim is a compulsory cross-claim. (CONCLUSION)

You should be able to tie each point directly to your conclusion. If you cannot do so, you probably do not need that point in your memo. In the example, are there any points that do not belong? Points 4 and 5 discuss an exception regarding claims brought in state court that does not apply to your facts because your case does not involve a state court claim. Thus, you can remove those points from your document. If the state court exception is discussed at all, the discussion should be extremely short because it is not relevant to your conclusion.

These sorts of tangents often appear when a writer follows the case law, rather than the facts of his or her own case. If most of the relevant cases discuss an issue, it can be easy to write about it, but that does not mean it belongs in the document. A legal document is rarely just a survey or regurgitation of everything in the case law. Instead, the legal writer's job is to pull out the parts of the cases that are germane to the facts of the particular case being analyzed.

While you are being cutthroat in deleting unnecessary points, make sure to save them in a separate document. I like to call this document "scraps." Your scraps document is an island of misfit ideas. By saving these ideas, you can come back and harvest your hard work later. You might end up needing the scraps for another document, or the reviewing attorney might ask you to replace something in the final draft with one of the parts that you put into your scraps document. Saving your irrelevant, albeit beloved, points in a separate document (rather than just deleting them forever) will make the streamlining process less painful.

## 4. Build a Bunker

Collecting all the non-essential ideas into a scraps document will allow you to prioritize the most important issues in your main document. Your main document is now more like a snake (yuck), than an octopus (also yuck). Once your main document is de-complicated, you can move the best of the scraps into a bunker inside your main document made up of comments, questions, and footnotes. A bunker is critical for survival. You put things in the bunker that will help you survive, including canned goods, water, weapons, and in the case of a legal document, any issues that you feel need to be brought to a senior attorney's attention.

Look back at your scraps. Make the most important of those ideas into footnotes in your main document. You do not want your document to look like a law review article, but it is fine to have a few useful footnotes. I prefer no more than three footnotes in a ten-page document, but this is a matter of taste and can vary widely. A footnote can be a great place to distinguish adverse authority, to discuss a cited case in more detail, or to make a subtle point about the conduct of opposing counsel. In fact, sometimes the senior attorney reviewing your document ends up liking one of the footnotes so much that he or she suggests putting it in the body of your document.

Make any other scraps that are nagging at you into internal comments or questions in the margin of your main document. Sometimes when you exercise your judgment in de-complicating a document, you are left with information that did not make it into the document, but raises issues that the person reviewing the document should know. For example, you may have an argument that is supported by a case that is factually and legally similar to your position, but the general weight of the authority goes the other way. You can insert a carefully worded comment or question that concisely describes the issue and flags it for the person reviewing the document. Doing so will clear your conscience and show the reviewing attorney your effort to exercise good judgment in resolving the issue on your own.

As with footnotes, you want your internal comments and questions to be very limited. Try to only write comments or questions about issues where you think reasonable minds could differ about your approach. If your document is loaded up with too many comments or questions, the reviewing attorney may think that you did not sufficiently think through the issues. You want any comment or question to be worth the reviewing attorney's time. The best comments and questions will make you look like a champ for spotting potential problems and bringing them to the reviewing attorney's attention.

Depending on the personality of the attorney you work with, you may want to discuss your comments and questions in person or on the phone, instead of building a bunker. Although it can sometimes be scary, talking things over is often the most efficient way to resolve the issues that are complicating a document. Also, asking good questions and raising thoughtful concerns can make you look like a hero. By doing it in person, you will get a chance to impress the attorney who is reviewing your document. Be brave enough to grab the bull (or shark, zombie, bear, alien, ape, werewolf, rhinoceros, whatever) by the horns!

## C. How to Shorten a Document That Is Too Long

Legal documents are like campfire stories. They lose all of their charm when they drag on for too long. Is your document longer than the page limit? If there is no page limit, does your document bore you? Legal readers can be impatient, and nobody enjoys reading a document that is longer than it needs to be.

Follow these three steps to revise your document and make it shorter: 1) travel light by revising anything longer than it needs to be, removing any repetition, and deleting any unhelpful citations, 2) travel smart by applying proper grammar and good writing principles, and 3) know the lay of the land by looking closely at the formatting of your document.

## 1. Travel Light

Like the survivor who fashions a fishing line from a shoelace, writing an effective and concise legal document requires making do with less.[10] You do not want to have a document that is any longer than it needs to be.

First, if your document is already simplified, but needs to be shorter, look for any sentences, paragraphs, sections, sub-sections, or parentheticals in your document that look longer than the others. Anything that looks long is ripe for shortening.

Next, look for repetition. Read every paragraph carefully and remove any sentences that repeat something that you have already said. You want to make each point so clearly that you only have to say it once. For example, do you have a point heading, a thesis sentence, and a conclusion sentence that all say the same thing? If so, try to shorten the point heading, keep the thesis, and delete or truncate the conclusion.

Last, take a hard look at all of your citations. Citations dramatically increase the length of your document. Make sure that every citation and parenthetical explanation adds value to your document. Long string citations do not do much for the reader, and they make your document much longer. Only include citations that add something of value to your document.

## 2. Travel Smart

Proper grammar and the principles of good writing are like keeping your feet dry and wearing sunscreen; they are always a good idea if you are trying to survive. But this is especially true when it comes to making your document shorter. You want to employ any and all grammar and good writing tips that will allow you to remove bulk from your document.

Here are some of the most common document-lengthening legal writing issues:

- **Adjectives and adverbs.** Dramatic adjectives and adverbs stand out to the reader and often seem out of

---

10. Your long document might be an overly complicated document in disguise. If so, try the steps in Chapter I, Section B on how to simplify a document that is too complicated.

place. Deleting most of them will save you space. For example, if adjectives like "baseless," "meritless," and "outrageous," or adverbs like "clearly," "plainly," and "obviously" appear throughout your document, you can probably save some space by removing them.

- **Passive voice.** Passive voice is a sentence construction where the object of the sentence replaces the subject. Look for passive voice (the word "by" in the sentence is often a giveaway) and make it active. You will save a few words almost every time you make this change.
- **Sentences that start with "this" or "it."** These vague words often indicate that your sentence starts with a non-essential phrase. The worst offenders are phrases like, "it is important to note that...," or "this means that...." Removing these non-essential introductory phrases will make your sentences shorter.
- **"In order."** This phrase rarely adds anything of substance. You can just delete it. Two words saved every time!
- **Nominalizations.** Making verbs into nouns usually adds length to your sentences. Words that end with "ment" or "ion," like "agreement," or "indication," are often nominalizations. Make the noun into a verb, like "agree," or "indicate," and you will often shorten your sentence.

## 3. Know the Lay of the Land

Formatting can have a major impact on the length of a document. By making a few formatting changes, you may save some critical space in a document that is too long.

The first thing you need to do is format everything properly. You want your document to have the right font, proper margins, and page numbers. Be careful that you do not make any formatting changes that will violate the rules governing your document in an effort to make your document shorter. For example, many local rules establish the margins that you have to use in your document. Thus, monkeying around with the margins, like you may have done in college, is not a smart idea. A document that is under the page limit, but does not follow the local rules is not going to do you any good. Once you have confirmed that your document is properly formatted, try to save space with these tips.

- **Point headings.** Revise your point headings so that they are only one or two lines, and make sure all of your point headings are single spaced.
- **Stubby lines.** Look for lines of text with only a few words. Try to revise the preceding sentences to delete enough words to move things up a line. When your document is too long, every line counts.
- **Widow/orphan control.** Consider turning off the widow/orphan settings in your document, which alter the page breaks to avoid stranding the first or last line of a paragraph. Because the widow control prevents the first line of a paragraph from being stranded on a page by itself, and the orphan control prevents the last line of a paragraph from being stranded, this setting often increases your document's page count by moving text on to the next page.
- **Shorten defined terms.** Revisit any defined terms. If you have a party or term in the case with a long defined name, think about defining it to be something shorter. For example, if you repeatedly refer to your client as "The Supreme Leader of the Future Colony of Mars," rather than Ms. Jones, or just Jones, you are going to be using up a lot of space throughout your document.
- **Footnotes.** Experiment with the placement of any footnotes. Due to the mysteries of document formatting, one footnote in the wrong place can make the document much longer because it puts white space before the bottom of the page.

Try to enjoy the process of shortening your legal documents. Think like Ernest Hemingway—a tough guy who survived the Spanish Civil War and never wasted a word.

# D. How to Figure Out a Document That You Do Not Understand

You have been assigned a writing project. It seems very important. And yet, you do not understand what you are supposed to do. Although it sounds strange, this situation is very common. Do not be embarrassed; there is hope.

If you happen to work for someone who is available, accessible, and willing to answer questions, then just ask him or her to clarify what you are supposed to be doing. But if you work for someone who is maybe not so approachable, or you fear that your question will make you look like a doofus, you can still figure out this document that you do not understand.

Follow these three steps when you do not understand your document: 1) conduct reconnaissance by identifying what you are confused about, 2) resist the impulse to write an email full of random questions, and 3) send up smoke signals by asking the right people good questions.

## 1. Conduct Reconnaissance

First, identify the source of your confusion. Create a list of the issues or questions that have you bewildered. Do you not understand the purpose of the document? Are you confused about the facts? Are you uncertain of the procedural posture? Do you need help identifying the applicable law?

You should try to identify clear, succinct questions that you need answered to be able to write your document. For example, rather than formulating a question like this:

> What is the deal with these discovery disputes?

You are better off with a question like this:

> How can we file an opposition to Plaintiff's motion to compel the production of documents when we have agreed to produce the requested documents?

Identifying the specific information that you need to understand the document will make it much easier for you to figure out what the document is supposed to be about. It will also allow you to ask questions that show you have made a good-faith effort to answer your questions before seeking a clarification from a senior attorney, rather than asking questions willy-nilly.

## 2. Resist

Now that you have your list of specific questions, you may be inclined to dash off a long email to a senior attorney listing all of these questions and asking for help. Please, for just a moment, resist the siren song of that email. I am begging you.

No one likes to get a huge email asking for the answers to a million detailed questions. I know because many of my students send me just that kind of email the night before a big assignment is due. I watch the emails pop up in my inbox and my heart fills with dread.

Here is an example of the kind of painful (for both the sender and the recipient) email that I am talking about:

**From:** Junior Attorney
**Sent:** Hours Before Memo is Due
**To:** Senior Attorney
**Subject:** Memo Questions

Hello,

I have been working on the memo, and I have a couple quick questions. They are listed below. Thanks for your help!

1)  For formatting, does the memo have to be left justified or can it be fully justified, which I think looks better?
2)  In the facts section, can I assume the facts described in the complaint? For example, should I accept it as true that Plaintiff suffered economic harm?
3)  I don't understand this memo. Why am I writing a memo analyzing this issue under Florida law when

it appears that this issue is governed by a federal statute? Shouldn't the memo describe the federal statute and the way that it has been interpreted by the Eleventh Circuit?

4) I was wondering if it was OK to separate my rules into more than one paragraph? With the parentheticals and the amount of rules, it makes the paragraph quite long.

5) When referring to the Supreme Court of Florida is the C capitalized? Or is that just for the United States Supreme Court?

6) Do you think it is worth researching and discussing related criminal statutes or should I just stick to the civil claims?

7) Is the period at the end of a statute citation mandatory, or is it only for when the citation is at the end of a sentence? For example, if my citation is in the middle of a sentence, can I leave off the period?

Have a good evening, and thanks for answering these questions on such short notice!

Junior Attorney

You should not send an email like this. In the abstract, these questions are not particularly objectionable. And they probably would not take the recipient that much time to answer.

So why is sending this email a bad idea? First, you can tell that the sender did not do everything in his or her power to find the answers to these questions. There may be legitimate substantive questions posed in this email, but the sender could have easily answered some of these questions, like questions 5 and 7, by using The Bluebook. You do not want senior attorneys to think that you are trying to pass off your work to them. You have to make a good faith effort to answer questions on your own before asking someone else.

Second, the questions in the email are scattered. Some are very narrow, like questions 1 and 2, while others are very broad, like questions 3 and 6. This disorganization makes it look as though the sender is really floundering. But even if he or she *was* really floundering, it would be better to convey in the email that the sender tried to find alternative sources to answer these questions. An email like this conveys that the junior attorney cannot handle the assignment, which could lead the senior attorney to lose trust in that junior attorney.

Last, this email is too long. We should all aspire to send shorter emails. This is especially true now that we all read our emails on our phones while we are doing a thousand other things.

## 3. Send Up Smoke Signals

Ultimately, you may need to send an email that asks a few targeted questions. But your goal has to be to write an email that is short, necessary, and well organized. To do this, you have to start with due diligence so that you answer as many questions on your own as possible.

If your confusion is factual or logistical, try to get as much background as possible. Look for prior emails discussing the assignment, relevant documents from the case file, or notes from the meeting where the project was assigned. If similar or related documents have already been written in your case, review them. If the senior attorney has assigned other junior attorneys to write similar documents in the past, find those documents because they will be helpful examples.

If you are confused about the law or procedure, locate a treatise or practice guide on the subject. Google anything you can. Re-read the main cases. Look for cases that cite those cases or cases cited within those cases. If you have a statute, look through the annotations. And again, try to find similar documents that have been written in your case or in other cases that you can use as examples.

As you learn useful information, cross off the questions on your list that you have answered. This process should help you narrow down your confusion to something very specific.

You have now done your due diligence, so it is safe to ask someone else for help. As you probably know, most law offices are hierarchical. In my experience, the people in the lower tiers are often more approachable than the big-time bosses at the top.[11]

When you need to ask a potentially embarrassing question, you want to start with the least scary person possible. This could be a law librarian, a paralegal, another junior attorney, or any other colleague whom you feel comfortable asking for help. Respect this person's time and ask your questions as succinctly as possible. If you ask your questions by email, make the email organized and brief. And always be grateful for any help you receive.

You will be amazed by the number of questions that you can get answered this way. Cross any question off your list that gets answered by the first nice person you ask. And if you still have questions, work your way up the hierarchy of seniority, asking your carefully considered questions until you sort out your confusion. Each time you ask a new person, make sure to tell him or her (briefly) everything that you have done to answer the question for yourself, so it is clear that you are inquiring only out of necessity. Eventually, you may end up asking a senior attorney a few of your questions. That is OK because if you have followed the smoke signals process, you will be asking that senior attorney the questions that only he or she can answer.

At some point, there should be no more questions on your list. Or maybe, there are a few questions that have no answer. In either case, once most of your questions are answered, you have to start writing. You cannot let the quest to find a perfect answer to every question put off the writing process indefinitely. When you cannot find the trail you are looking for in the woods, sometimes the best thing to do is just start walking in the right direction. So, get to it!

---

11. Obviously, your experience may vary based on the personalities and structures where you work. I like imagining a law office where the sweet senior partners are terrorized by impatient paralegals, but I have not seen it yet.

# Chapter II

# Surviving Memos

Memos can be deceiving when it comes to survival. Because memos are usually objective, or at least semi-objective, they lack the drama and excitement of sexier forms of legal writing like persuasive briefs. But that does not mean that every memo is going to be a walk in the park. Sometimes, writing a memo is like taking a walk in the park and then getting attacked by a scurry[1] of rabid squirrels.

Memos live forever. You have to think of your memo as a time capsule that preserves what you knew at a particular moment. Because someone can always dig one of your old memos out of the file, you want each memo to be self-contained. The three hallmarks of a good memo are as follows:

1) accuracy,
2) thoroughness, and
3) readability.

First, a memo must be accurate about the facts and law it relies upon. A memo based on inaccurate information is as useful as a map of the moon when you are trying to get to Katz's Delicatessen on the Lower East Side.

Second, a memo must be thorough. Information that does not make it into a memo risks being lost or overlooked. Cases can last a long time. A memo may stay with a case longer than you do, so you cannot count on the person reading it to have the same background information that you had. As people come and go, the institutional knowledge of a case or matter can get lost or be forgotten.

---

1. A "scurry" is the name for a pack of squirrels. Go ahead, Google it.

The only way to preserve institutional knowledge is to explicitly include it in your memo.

Last, like all of your legal writing, you want any memo to be readable. A well-written memo is easy to understand. It is also easy to convert into other documents, like letters, emails, and even briefs. This chapter offers strategies for common memo problems. If you have a memo that is chasing you down like a hungry bear, read on for tips for how to survive.

## A. The Memo That Could Not Find the "Right" Answer

Lawyers do not write memos in a vacuum. They also do not write memos in a vacuum cleaner. (Thank goodness! The dust! The noise!) Lawyers write memos while representing clients. And typically, those memos mean something to those clients.

It would be fabulous if every memo confirmed that your client is the good guy and things are going to work out swimmingly. But what happens when your memo reaches a conclusion that is not so great for your client? Nobody likes bad news. So when that happens, you need to take steps to reduce the upset caused by your memo.

Follow these three steps to navigate a memo that did not find the "right" answer: 1) use dead reckoning to verify that your conclusion is correct, 2) consider escape options offered by counterarguments and creative recommendations, and 3) avoid sneak attacks through careful public relations.

### 1. Use Dead Reckoning[2]

If you have reached a conclusion that is not favorable for your client, the first thing to do is make sure that your conclusion is cor-

---

2. Dead reckoning is a kind of navigation where you calculate the current position of a plane or ship by using its last known position and its estimated speed and direction. If you decide to become a pirate, this definition will likely be important. For a lawyer, not so much.

rect. You do not want to get everyone riled up over an incorrect conclusion. Remember: it is absolutely not your fault if your research results in an answer that the powers-that-be are not jazzed about. But if you lack confidence in your conclusion, you will make a ton of work for yourself. The first thing any senior attorney is going to do is challenge the basis for your unpopular conclusion. Then, you will just have to go back and re-check your work anyway. So why not make sure you are right before that happens? Double checking your conclusion will prepare you to face the firing squad of attorneys who will hope that you are wrong.

To double check your work, you need to go back to the beginning. This means pulling out all of the legal and factual authorities you used to write your memo and checking everything for accuracy. Do not do this from memory! You need to actually look at the documents with your eyeballs.

Then, you need to imagine that you are sitting with a very skeptical senior attorney who is cross-examining you about your conclusion. Doing this will help you anticipate and prepare for all of the difficult questions that might come your way. For example,

- Are the legal authorities you rely upon still good law?
- Have you updated your research to find any new cases?
- Do you feel certain that you have found all of the relevant authorities?
- Have you verified the accuracy of your facts in the record documents?
- Is there any way to credibly distinguish the unfavorable cases?

Going through this process is good for you. It is insurance that your conclusion is the right one. And if it turns out that you were wrong, kudos to you for catching the mistake now, before anyone else knew about it.

## 2. Consider Escape Options

Your client is counting on you to do accurate legal analysis. An artificially rose-colored view does not help anyone. But if your conclusion is unfavorable, you want to demonstrate that you are on your client's side. How do you do this? By offering solutions in your memo. When the other avalanche survivor asks you if his toes look frostbitten, you need to be the person who says yes and then offers to cut them off with a machete, rather than the person who says that they look fine and then starts walking faster in the hope of losing the guy before the wolves show up.

First, you need to thoroughly consider possible counterarguments and rebuttals in the course of your discussion. For each argument you identify that is bad for your client, you want to think about whether there are any counterarguments that are good for your client. You want to provide your client with any feasible counterarguments, even if they do not change your ultimate conclusion. For example, if there is a bad case for your side, think about whether there are any bases to distinguish it, and if there are, include them. Similarly, if there are any counterarguments that allow you to limit the impact of a bad fact, include those arguments in your memo. Then, you need to consider whether there are any rebuttals to your counterarguments. Think of yourself as both the hardened skeptic who is focused on the bad news, and the lighthearted optimist who has not given up hope.

Next, try to provide recommendations to get around the unfavorable conclusion. Be creative. Consider whether there is evidence that you could look for, procedures that you could invoke, or steps that you could take that would minimize the negative effects of your conclusion. Again, you want to make it clear in your memo that despite its less than ideal outcome, you have considered all of the possible solutions for your client.

Recommend strategic options, practical solutions, and anything favorable to your client that could mitigate the unfavorable conclusion. For example, imagine that you have written a memo that concludes that your opponent will likely prevail on a motion to dismiss. That is bad news. But your memo could suggest stipulating with the opposing party to amend the complaint to correct whatever defect makes the motion to dismiss likely to succeed. Your memo could also conclude that the amended complaint would probably not be vulnerable to another motion to dismiss. This recommendation would balance your memo's unfavorable conclusion with something positive for your client.

Offering a creative recommendation is not just good for your client; it is good for you too. It shows that you appreciate the seriousness of your conclusion and that you are invested in helping your client deal with it. Often, junior attorneys are insulated from case strategy. By offering solutions, you show that you are able and willing to be involved in the higher-level decisions on a case, which makes you look like a champ. And being a champ is good for your client and your career.

## 3. No Sneak Attacks

The last survival step for handling a memo that did not find the "right" answer relates to public relations. You do not want your unfavorable conclusion to come as a surprise to people who matter. Meeting a bear in the woods is not a great situation, but surprising a bear in the woods is even worse. You want to leave a trail of bad news crumbs, so that the senior attorney reviewing your memo will not be shocked to learn that you did not find the answer that everyone was hoping for.

There are two ways to make sure that your memo is not a sneak attack. First, once you have done enough analysis to know — for sure — that the answer is not looking good for your client, you might want to leak your conclusion to a senior attorney. A well-timed leak will mean that your completed memo will not be like an Earth-destroying meteor that no scientist predicted. Second, be savvy about who is responsible for communicating the unfortunate conclusion to the client. You want your client to learn the news in the least distressing way possible. Minimizing the shock caused by your unfavorable conclusion is the best way to avert any blaming of the messenger (meaning, you).

# B. The Memo That Could Not Reach a Conclusion

Lawyers do not write memos for the fun of it.[3] As you know, lawyers write memos to analyze legal problems and offer advice based on their analysis. Because memos are not just an academic exercise, they need to provide conclusions that can be used to make real decisions. Writing a memo that does not reach a conclusion is like surviving a plane crash and then complaining about the in-flight meal. It misses the whole point.

Reaching a conclusion can be difficult because a memo is usually assigned when a legal issue lacks an easy answer. Resolving those close calls is the very purpose of writing a memo.

Here is what you should do when you are faced with a no-conclusion conundrum: 1) get a compass by channeling a normal person, 2) find true north by identifying your thesis, 3) make a map of the outcomes of the relevant cases, and 4) weigh tactical considerations, including what conclusion would be best for your client.

## 1. Get a Compass

When working on a memo, it is easy to lose perspective. Losing perspective is like being lost in the woods. Every twig starts to look like every other twig, and all the paths take you back to where you started. As you write a memo, you can get so wrapped up in the case law that you no longer think like a normal person. Channeling a regular human being is often the best way to figure out the most logical conclusion for your memo. A normal person's perspective can serve as your compass.

Imagine someone normal in your life—someone who has good-old common sense. This person probably is not a lawyer. I mean,

---

3. Fun is just an awesome byproduct of the memo writing process.

how many normal lawyers do you know? Now consider whether your conclusion would sound completely ridiculous to this civilian. For example, imagine telling your mother,[4]

> *I have concluded that my client is likely guilty of aggravated assault because he yelled at his neighbor while holding a soup ladle, and a soup ladle can be classified as a deadly weapon.*

Although this conclusion might make sense to you after you have been buried for weeks in cases that broadly define a deadly weapon, to our normal person this conclusion sounds completely ridiculous. Your conclusion does not pass the straight-face test. Whenever possible, you want to avoid taking a position that is so "out there" that it would amuse a normal person.

## 2. Find True North

Running your argument by your normal person serves another important purpose aside from the straight-face test. It forces you to isolate and describe your memo's possible conclusions. Often, a memo that cannot reach a conclusion is really just a memo that does not have a clear thesis. Nothing dooms a piece of legal writing like the lack of a thesis. You cannot come back from it. A memo without a thesis is like a compass that cannot find true north.

If you do not have a thesis sentence, you need to write one right now. This very second.[5] If the issue is so close that you cannot decide what your thesis should be, write out both potential thesis sentences. Then try them on like hiking boots. Writing a memo with a thesis that you ultimately decide is wrong, so that you have to go

---

4. This is assuming that your mother is a normal person. My mother definitely does not fall into this category, so I would have to choose someone else. Indeed, my mother reads so many crime novels that she considers herself an amateur district attorney. She would probably already know the law on aggravated assault before I told her about my soup-ladle-wielding client.

5. Chapter I, Section B, Part 1 offers help for writing thesis sentences.

back and revise the memo to support the opposite conclusion, is better than writing a wishy-washy memo with no thesis at all.

## 3. Make a Map

Often the key to survival is having a good map. One way to reach a conclusion on a close call is to map the outcomes of all the similar, relevant cases. Try making a chart that lists the outcome of each case. If all or most of the similar cases tend to come out one way, that conclusion is more likely than the other.

Here is a sample chart mapping the outcomes of cases[6] relating to whether an object constituted a deadly weapon for purposes of aggravated assault:

### Figure 1. Case Outcome Map.

| Citation | Facts | Outcome |
|---|---|---|
| *Smith v. Smith*, 100 F.3d 100 (13th Cir. 2001). | Victim was attacked with a butter knife. | Deadly weapon. |
| *Jones v. Jones*, 200 F.3d 200 (14th Cir. 2002). | Defendant brandished a crab fork in a threatening manner. | Not a deadly weapon. |
| *Lee v. Lee*, 300 F.3d 300 (15th Cir. 2003). | Defendant struck victim with a teaspoon. | Not a deadly weapon. |

The map method can help you see the trend of decisions on a particular issue, especially when you have a bunch of cases from different, non-binding jurisdictions. It can also be a good way to break a tie when you do not feel strongly about either outcome.

But please remember that you really only need one legally and factually similar case from a relevant jurisdiction to support your argument. Even if most of the cases come out the other way, you

---

6. Again, please do not use this book for any substantive law. I have made these cases up.

can support your conclusion with one good case that is similar to your own. Your map can help you decide a close call, but reaching a sound legal conclusion is more than a numbers game.

## 4. Weigh Tactical Considerations

If your memo is truly a close call with law that supports either conclusion, choose the outcome that helps your client. It is that simple. You should not just tell your clients what they want to hear. But you should be an advocate who wants to find favorable conclusions for your clients. Thus, if one reasonable conclusion is good for your client and the other is not, go ahead and lean toward the positive outcome.

When you have had a difficult time reaching a conclusion, you should let your reader know that it is a close call, while still reaching a conclusion one way or the other. Let your memo reflect the balanced analysis that led to your conclusion and include all of the relevant facts, rules, and arguments for both sides. Describe in detail the points that weigh against your conclusion, and let your reader know the places where reasonable minds could differ.

Deluding yourself will not help you to survive either legal writing or the wilderness. So do not write a close call like it is a slam-dunk. Couching your conclusion and thoroughly describing all of the relevant arguments and counterarguments will allow your reader to have enough information to make his or her own evaluation.

# Chapter III

# Surviving Briefs

Writing a good brief really comes down to one thing: doing everything possible to convince the court that you should prevail.[1] To evaluate the effectiveness of your brief, you need to stand in the shoes of your reader. Or, more accurately, you need to sit in the big leather chair that is behind the fancy desk, turn on the old-fashioned banker's lamp, dip your quill into the inkpot,[2] and imagine that you are the judge who is going to decide which party is going to win.

To persuade a judge, an effective brief needs to be

1) focused,
2) organized, and
3) confident.

First, you want your brief to be focused on what is relevant. Cases get complicated. There can be secondary, tertiary, and quaternary legal issues that come up in a case. Plus, grudges, slights, and all kinds of bad blood can develop between the parties. You do not want to put any of that in a brief when it is not relevant. Discussing issues that are outside the scope of the brief will irritate the court, waste valuable words and pages on issues that will not help you win, and may even hurt your case or client.

Second, you need to deploy a clear, logical organizational scheme. Your argument should unfold so logically that the reader expects what

---

1. For the sake of simplicity, this chapter will use the term "brief" to refer to any kind of persuasive legal document that is directed to a court.

2. This is not really what most judges' chambers look like. But because we are imagining, we might as well go all out.

is going to come next. The best way to do this is through persuasive point headings and close adherence to the CRAC format. Also,
you should make sure that your well-organized brief *looks* organized. You know the saying, "don't judge a book by its cover"? Every
judge will do exactly that. You want the judge to like your brief, so
make it look like a winner. You can do this by

- making your formatting consistent and in compliance
  with the local rules;
- avoiding all capital letters whenever possible;[3]
- moving any orphaned headings from the bottom of one
  page to the top of the next page;
- italicizing, bolding, and underlining sparingly; and
- including page numbers.

Last, your document should have a confident tone, without
being smug. You can accomplish this through careful word choice
and argument selection. The words you use and the arguments you
present should be appropriate and fair. You want to sound like
someone who knows what he or she is talking about and not like
a jerk. When you read your own brief, the experience should make
you like yourself. If, when you read your own brief, you want to feed
the author to the wolves, there is probably some work to do on the
tone of your document.

This chapter offers strategies for common brief problems. If a
brief is giving you fits like a swarm of mosquitoes, read on for survival tips.

## A. The Brief That Deals with Bad Facts

Facts matter. Every lawyer will at some point have to prepare a
document that has to dance around some pretty ugly facts. Mini-

---

3. ALL CAPS CAN BE HARD TO READ. YOU PROBABLY KNOW
THIS INSTINCTIVELY, EVEN IF YOU HAVE NEVER REALLY GIVEN
IT MUCH THOUGHT. See?

mizing the impact of bad facts is one of a lawyer's super powers. When writing a brief that involves bad facts, you want to do everything you can to minimize the impact those facts will have on the court's decision.

Here are three steps that will help you handle bad facts: 1) scout out the source documents to confirm that the bad facts are as bad as you think they are, 2) avoid freaking out over the bad facts until you are sure they are relevant, and 3) camouflage the bad facts through re-branding, sandwiching, and sheltering.

## 1. Scout

First, verify that any bad fact is actually as bad as you think it is. Check different factual sources to identify the best version of a bad fact. For example, multiple deponents may describe a key event. You want to present only the best possible version of any bad fact, without changing or omitting relevant information.

## 2. Do Not Freak Out

Second, confirm that each bad fact is relevant to your motion. A bad fact can be overwhelming. But you only have to talk about a bad fact if it is legally relevant.

## 3. Camouflage

Third, if you have to deal with a bad fact, you need to camouflage it until it is almost invisible. Camouflage is one of your best survival skills whether you are hiding from a horde of zombies or dealing with a bad fact.

### a. Rebrand the Slimeheads

Often, minimizing a bad fact requires nothing more than changing your vocabulary. In the 1980s, a fish called the orange roughy became a popular dish. So popular, in fact, that even my parents were into it.[4] The orange roughy's popularity was largely attributed to a name change. Before it was called the orange roughy, people knew this fish as the "slimehead." Needless to say, there was not much interest among my parents or anyone else in eating the slimehead.

The same thing can happen with facts. A bad fact is a slimehead that you need to re-brand. As long as your description remains factually accurate, there is nothing stopping you from re-branding a bad fact. Accordingly, you should avoid adopting slimeheads from documents prepared by the other side or the depositions of unfavorable witnesses. You do not have to accept your opponent's unfavorable description of a bad fact. You have the freedom to use different language to describe a bad fact in a way that is better for your side.

One of the best ways to re-brand a bad fact is to change the level of specificity used to describe it. Depending on the bad fact, getting more general or more specific can make it seem like less of a big deal. It is the feeling you get when you are looking out the window from a high floor in a tall building and all the people below look like bugs, or when you see a photo of a fly that has been so magnified that you can see every hair on its head. Thinking about the level of specificity can help you get some perspective on a bad fact.

For example, imagine that you have a client who has been sued for breach of contract for not fulfilling an order that was made by the plaintiff. The order was for a variety of woolen goods, including hats, scarves, sweaters, and mittens. Your client provided the hats, scarves, and sweaters, but could not fulfill the order for mittens. The plaintiff in that case would want to refer to the "mitten contract." But you would want to take a more general view and refer to the "woolen goods contract." By being less specific, you have re-branded the "mitten" slimehead and changed the vocabulary to help your client.

---

4. My parents are not on the cutting edge of seafood eating.

## b. Make Sandwiches

Once you have adopted a better vocabulary for your bad facts, think about matching up every bad fact with countervailing good facts. By attaching your bad facts to better facts, you will be able to minimize how bad those facts seem to the reader. Sandwiches are important in any survival situation, and one of the best ways to minimize a bad fact is to make a sandwich where the good facts are the bread and the bad fact is the bologna. This way, every bad fact is smooshed between two better facts, de-emphasizing its significance. Like this:

**Figure 2. Bad Fact Sandwich.**

A chart can help you match up your good and bad facts to make these sandwiches. In my view, a chart can solve almost every problem.[5] And bad facts are no exception. For example, if you had to

---

5. Obviously, I have not tried out this chart theory with every conceivable problem. For example, I cannot promise you that a chart will solve problems like alien invasions, shark attacks, avalanches, or flesh-eating viruses. But I would not be surprised if a chart turned out to be very helpful in those situations.

write a motion to compel the defendant to produce documents, you could make a chart like this:

**Figure 3. Good and Bad Facts Chart for Motion to Compel.**

| Relevance | Good Facts | Bad Facts |
| --- | --- | --- |
| Evidence of whether we have been diligent in attempting to obtain documents. | Requested documents in first set of requests for production. | Did not follow up on request for three months. |
| Evidence that Defendant has not complied with discovery obligations. | Defendant only produced documents responsive to 5 out of 20 requests. | We agreed to limit some of our requests because they were too broad. |
| Evidence that Defendant has not yet produced all relevant documents. | Defendant's witness admitted at deposition that there were more relevant documents that have not been collected or produced.<br><br>Despite this, Defendant has not supplemented its production. | Those additional documents do not fit neatly within any of our requests. |

Once you have your chart, the sandwiches practically make themselves.[6] You simply match up the facts that make sense together, putting the good facts at the beginning and the end and the bad facts in the middle. Here are the bad fact sandwiches for the chart above:

> Plaintiff requested the documents at issue in its first set of requests for production. (**GOOD**) When Plaintiff followed up three months later, it agreed to limit the breadth of some requests. (**BAD**) Defendant only produced documents responsive to five out of twenty requests. (**GOOD**)

---

6. Can you imagine? What could be better than sandwiches that make themselves?

Defendant's witness admitted at deposition that there are more relevant documents that have not been collected or produced. **(GOOD)** Some of these relevant, additional documents are not explicitly covered by Plaintiff's first requests for production. **(BAD)** Although there are relevant documents that have not been produced, Defendant has not supplemented its production. **(GOOD)**

In both paragraphs above, the bad facts are sandwiched between good facts. By doing so, the good facts are emphasized and the bad facts are de-emphasized.

### c. Seek Shelter

Shelter is critical for survival. When you are exposed to the elements, it is easy for predators to find you (and eat you for dinner). The same is true for bad facts in your brief. To minimize a bad fact, you need to shelter it so that it is not so obvious to the reader. Here is a bright-line rule: A bad fact should never be at the very beginning or the very end of a section or paragraph. Legal readers usually pay the most attention to text that is near white space, so you want your bad facts to be as far away from white space as possible. This is another benefit of a bad fact sandwich. In a sandwich, the good facts keep your bad facts from being exposed when the reader is paying the most attention.

To see the impact of sandwiching and sheltering bad facts, read the following two fact paragraphs that are substantively identical, but organized differently. These fact paragraphs are for a brief filed on behalf of a criminal defendant who was charged with drug possession.

### FACTUAL BACKGROUND NO. 1

On June 5, 2011, Sam Smith was arrested for drug possession when he was found passed out on a street corner, holding a bag containing 1.8 grams of cocaine. He was covered in cuts and bruises. Smith is a well-respected teacher at Egret Community College. He is a member of numerous civic organizations and has never before been arrested or accused of any criminal wrongdoing. After he was given his *Miranda* warnings on June 5, Smith stated that he could not remember any specifics, but that he must have purchased the cocaine from one of his students.

### FACTUAL BACKGROUND NO. 2

Sam Smith is a well-respected teacher at Egret Community College. He is a member of numerous civic organizations and, before the present incident, had never been accused of any criminal wrongdoing or arrested. On June 5, 2011, Mr. Smith was found passed out on a street corner. The police arrested him for drug possession because he was holding a bag containing 1.8 grams of cocaine. After he was given his *Miranda* warnings, Mr. Smith stated that he must have purchased the cocaine from one of his students, but that he could not remember any specifics of what happened. Mr. Smith was covered in cuts and bruises.

These two paragraphs have the same substance, but give the reader a different impression of the facts. The first example puts the worst facts at the beginning and the end. It sandwiches the good facts between the bad facts and exposes the bad facts to white space. An organization like the one in the first paragraph highlights and emphasizes the bad facts. The second example sandwiches the bad facts between the good facts and shelters the bad facts away from the white space. The second example makes the bad facts less noticeable and highlights the good facts.

If you use these strategies to emphasize the good facts and minimize the bad facts, you will be a lawyer super hero.

# B. The Brief That Deals with Bad Law

The first time I ever went to the Everglades, I was walking along a path and suddenly there was an alligator blocking the way. The

alligator was in the middle of the path, sitting very still and hu-
mongous. He did not seem to be interested in me at all, but I think
we can all agree that from a survival perspective it would have been
dumb to pretend that he was not there and walk right into him.

The same goes for surviving a brief that has to deal with law that
supports your opponent's position, hurts your case, or otherwise
gives the court a reason to rule against you. In this situation, you
have to be an alligator-avoidance expert. And the first rule of effective
avoidance is to not ignore the alligator. Once you have accepted
that there is an alligator of bad law in your path, you can use the
steps below to survive.

There are two steps in dealing with bad law: 1) look for res-
cue by verifying your research, and 2) apply countermea-
sures by thinking like a problem solver, distinguishing the cases,
arguing that the bad cases were wrongly decided, and barricading
any weak distinguishing arguments in a footnote.

## 1. The Possibility of Rescue

As discussed in previous sections, before getting too upset about
your survival prospects in any legal writing situation, you want to
make sure that the situation is actually as bad as you think it is.
When you encounter bad law, you need to 1) make sure you understand the bad law, 2) confirm that the bad law is still valid, and
3) update your research to find any new good law that could help
you out.

First, make sure that you are reading and interpreting the bad law
correctly. Going back to the bad cases and reading them again is a good
place to start. You should also read the cases cited by the bad cases
for the bad points of law. Try and isolate the law that is particularly
bad for your brief and really understand it. Become an expert on this
bad law so that you can best decide what to do about it.

Second, verify that the bad law is still good law. Be thorough.
Check that the bad law has not been distinguished or — miracle of
miracles — overruled since you did your research. Follow all of the
negative citing references to see if they make any arguments that
you could use to show this bad law should not be followed.

Third, update your research to look for any new decisions that help your side. Run your searches again. When there is bad law out there, you should continually look for good cases that go your way. Although it might seem highly unlikely that a magical case would get decided rejecting the bad law that is causing you so much trouble, imagine how dopey you would feel if that happened and you did not know about it. Cases get decided all the time. Do not give up hope that a useful decision could appear at any moment.

Last, if you have any spare pennies, you might as well throw them into the nearest fountain with a wish for some good authority.

## 2. Countermeasures

### a. Adopt a Problem-Solving Mindset

When it comes to bad news and bad law, there are two kinds of people (and two kinds of lawyers): problem identifiers and problem solvers. A problem identifier can find problems anywhere. Beach vacation? Sunburn. Generous gift? Guilt. Pastrami sandwich? Indigestion.

Problem identifiers can be great lawyers. They think through all of the ways a contract, a strategy, or a phone call can go wrong. They warn their clients about hidden traps and unintended consequences. They are just the people you want to have around when you are deciding whether to make a choice that has a big downside, but a huge potential upside. In a survival situation, your problem identifier is the guy who is going to warn you not to eat the berries because they could be poisonous.

But problem identifiers are not the best at distinguishing cases.[7] And when you have bad law, you have to distinguish it. To distinguish a bad case, you have to be a problem solver. You have to look at the bad case with a solutions-oriented mindset. Instead of ob-

---

7. They are also very annoying shoppers. Imagine trying to buy a sweater with someone who can only see the potential flaws in everything. "That sweater looks like it is made out of a house cat. That sweater is too thick for Florida weather. That sweater looks like something Bill Cosby would wear." It is maddening.

sessing about how the bad case dooms your argument, you have to find reasons why it is different from your case. Sometimes, you must anchor a distinguishing argument on the tiniest sliver that is barely there. If you are just a problem identifier, you will never see the sliver. You will be too distracted by all the ways the case is terrible for your brief.

To be a good distinguisher, you have to think like an optimistic problem solver. Problem solvers love finding solutions. They are the survivors who figure out how to turn a rain coat and an old shoe into a life raft. They can take any set of circumstances and see a favorable way out. When distinguishing cases, the bases for the distinction light up for a problem solver like they are written in neon.

### b. Outwit the Alligator

Now that you see yourself as a problem solver, you have to confront and outwit the alligator of bad law that is blocking the path of your brief. The following distinguishing techniques will help you make short work of bad law.

The most effective and efficient kind of distinguishing is when you can distinguish a bunch of cases all at the same time. Mass distinguishing allows you to rebut the bad law, while giving it minimal attention.

When mass distinguishing cases, I love the following sentence:

> All of the cases relied upon by [opponent] are inapposite because....

At the end of this sentence, you can explain, in a general way, why a whole mess of bad cases cannot possibly apply to your case. Then, you can list the cases with a parenthetical to briefly distinguish each one. It looks like this:

> All of the cases relied upon by Plaintiff are inapposite because they do not involve motions to dismiss under Rule 12(b)(6). *See, e.g., Smith v. Smith*, 100 F.3d 100, 101 (13th Cir. 2001) (denying a motion for summary judgment, not a motion to dismiss); *Jones v. Jones*, 200 F.3d 200, 202 (14th Cir. 2002) (granting a motion for

more definite statement); *Lee v. Lee*, 300 F.3d 300, 303 (15th Cir. 2003) (denying a motion for summary judgment brought by a plaintiff).

Here is another example of a mass distinguishing paragraph:

All of the cases relied upon by Plaintiff are inapposite because they were decided by courts outside of this jurisdiction, which apply a different standard for motions to dismiss. *See, e.g., Smith v. Smith*, 100 F.3d 100, 101 (13th Cir. 2001) (applying the law of the Thirteenth Circuit); *Jones v. Jones*, 200 F.3d 200, 202 (14th Cir. 2002) (applying the law of the Fourteenth Circuit); *Lee v. Lee*, 300 F.3d 300, 303 (15th Cir. 2003) (applying the law of the Fifteenth Circuit).

The only hard part about mass distinguishing is figuring out an overarching basis on which to distinguish the bad cases. As illustrated above, two of the best ways are 1) on a procedural basis, and 2) through the hierarchy of authority.

In the first mass distinguishing example, the bad cases have been distinguished on the procedural basis that they involved different types of motions than the motion at issue in that case. Thus, the distinguishing argument is that cases involving motions for summary judgment or a motion for more definite statement are not relevant to a decision on a motion to dismiss. If you can find a procedural reason like that one for why the bad cases differ from your case, and you can make a compelling argument about why that procedural difference is relevant, you have just successfully distinguished a bunch of cases.

In the second mass distinguishing example, the bad cases have been distinguished on the ground that they were decided by nonbinding courts. If you can argue that the bad cases are not relevant based on the hierarchy of authority, you have a golden distinguishing argument. Unfortunately, for this form of distinguishing to work, you have to be able to argue that the non-binding courts applied the law differently than the court should apply the law in your case. It is not enough to simply note that non-binding courts decided the cases. You have to show why the hierarchy of authority makes the cases distinguishable.

### c. Do What You Can

Sometimes when you have bad cases to distinguish, you have to distinguish them on their facts. Arguing that a case is not applicable to your case because it had different facts is a necessary evil. Although there are times when factual differences really do explain why a case is distinguishable, often this argument sounds like harping on irrelevant details. Every case is factually different from every other case. But many of the factual differences are so minor that they do not really matter.

To successfully distinguish a case on its facts, you have to make the factual differences seem important. Focus on the differences that can impact the court's decision by connecting the factual differences to a rule or legal standard. Otherwise, distinguishing facts that appear to be irrelevant makes your argument sound shallow.

For example, if you are trying to distinguish a breach of contract case from your own breach of contract case on the basis that the contracts were different, you only want to distinguish those differences that are legally relevant. That the contract in your case is for hiking boots and the contract in the other case was for backpacks is probably not going to help you because it is not tied to a legal standard that will determine the outcome of the case. But if the contract in your case has a condition precedent and the contract in the other case does not, that difference could be a useful basis for distinguishing because it may be legally relevant. The more you can make the distinguishable aspect a big deal, the better your factual distinguishing will be.

### d. Stand and Fight

There will be times when you do not have a strong basis to distinguish bad law. There might be a case that is so factually and legally similar to your case that you cannot find a way to argue it does not apply. This is not your fault. You are not to blame for the unfortunate state of the case law.

When you do not have a good distinguishing argument to make, you should consider the Hail Mary of distinguishing arguments: The bad case was wrongly decided. Rather than arguing that the bad case does not apply to your case, you can argue that the case should not apply because the court got that case wrong. This is the point at which you decide to just fight the alligator. Although fighting the alligator may seem nuts, crazier things have happened than a case being wrongly decided.[8]

If you decide to make this argument, you have to do so carefully. You do not want to offend the court. Making an argument that posits that you are smarter than whatever court decided the bad case can sound arrogant. Arrogance is probably not what you are going for when trying to convince a court to decide in your favor. To avoid sounding like a jerk, you need to be very aware of the tone of your stand and fight argument.[9]

Imagine that a case was wrongly decided. Now imagine explaining that to the court in a respectful and straight-forward way. Like this:

> The decision of *You v. Alligator* was wrongly decided, and is thus inapplicable here, for the following three reasons. First,…. Second,…. Third,….

This description of why the case was wrongly decided has credibility. Now imagine explaining in the most snarky and arrogant way possible that the case was wrongly decided:

> Obviously, the court's decision in *You v. Alligator* has no leg to stand on. That decision is improper on so many grounds that it is impossible to detail them all here.

---

8. For example, when I was growing up I had a cat who liked to eat corn on the cob.

9. If the wrongly decided case was decided by the same court, or even worse, the same judge who will decide your case, you have to be extremely careful about making this kind of argument. That situation makes an argument that is already a minefield especially treacherous.

That approach is not going to endear you to the court deciding your case because its tone suggests that you are not someone the court can trust. By adopting a reasonable and professional tone, you will have a better chance of making the court your ally when you decide to stand and fight an alligator of bad law.[10]

### e. Build a Barricade

The last option for distinguishing bad law is to do so in a footnote. By addressing the bad law in a footnote, you are signaling to the reader that the bad law is not important. A footnote can minimize the impact of the bad law by making the bad law appear incidental to the main point of your brief. It also isolates your weaker distinguishing arguments in a footnote where they should have less of an impact on your stronger arguments.

Be aware that, like any tactical decision, this footnote strategy can backfire. Your opponent may argue that you have failed to sufficiently address the bad law. This argument will go something like the following:

> Defendant has failed to adequately address the compelling authority cited by Plaintiff. Indeed, Defendant's only discussion of this authority occurs in a brief footnote.

Choosing whether to fight or build a barricade puts you in a tough spot. You have to make a strategic choice about which risk is worth taking. If you distinguish the cases in the text of your brief, you risk highlighting arguments that may sound weak. If you distinguish the cases in a footnote, you risk inviting the argument that you did not address them fully. To decide which option is the best, consider the strength of your distinguishing arguments and the importance of the bad cases to the outcome of the brief. Then, use your best survivalist judgment and live to fight another day.

---

10. I am not advising you to ever stand and fight an actual alligator. Please do not do that.

# Chapter IV

# Surviving Correspondence

Surviving correspondence is a daily project. Most of the writing that lawyers do is in the form of correspondence. This chapter focuses on email, but these survival tips apply to professional communication generally. They should help you to survive letters, text messages, and, in the future, hologram transmissions sent through a trashcan-shaped robot, and messages that you beam directly into the brain of your alien client waiting impatiently aboard the mother ship.

Effective professional correspondence has three qualities. It is

1) forthright,
2) sensitive, and
3) brief.

First, you want your correspondence to be forthright, meaning you want to be direct and get right to the point. You are writing to someone to tell him or her something, so you should do it. Lawyers have an impulse to correspond like they are serving in the court of King Henry VIII. You know the type: "Dearest Kindest Sir, I am writing to inform you that I will be travelling about the way and may approach your humble hearthstone about the morrow. Most sincere sincerities, Lord Cheringtonlislevillethameston." This is not necessary. Try instead, "I would like to meet tomorrow at 2 p.m." The more direct you are, the more effective your correspondence will be.

Second, you want your correspondence to be sensitive to the recipient. Any legal document needs to be attuned to its audience, but this is especially true of correspondence. Every email should have the proper tone for what it is trying to achieve. In some emails you may need to be stern, aggressive, or uncompromising, while in others you will need to be delicate, kind, or accommodating. The tone of any correspondence should be a conscious choice, not a consequence of the time you had to prepare the correspondence or the technology you used to do so.

Last, brevity is critical. No one likes to read long work emails. You want your correspondence to be as concise as possible. Now that so much correspondence is read on tiny little devices, a long email is likely an unread email. To understand how concise you need to be, you have to know your audience's tolerance for details. Many lawyers and business people do not have the time or the inclination to distill what is important from a long email. They want crisp, clear, and concise emails that get right to the point.

This chapter offers strategies for common correspondence issues. If you need to draft an email that is driving you crazier than a case of poison oak, keep reading for tips on how to survive.

## A. The "I Have Bad News" Email

Survival situations are not about everything working out perfectly. Indeed, most survival situations are about everything going wrong: the boat sinks, the plane crashes, the robots take over. Like any survivor, sometimes as a lawyer you have to tell someone bad news. Being the bearer of bad news is not a fun job. But giving bad news does not have to be so bad. There are ways to deliver bad news that will make it less painful for you and for the recipient. If you do it right, your bad news email will provide accurate information and demonstrate your value and competence.

The following three steps will help you effectively deliver bad news: 1) send a signal by choosing the right method of communication, 2) do first aid by choosing the proper tone, and 3) recover by offering an optimistic outlook.

### 1. Signal

When you have to pass along bad news, one of the first things you want to consider is the means of communication you will use.

As anyone who has ever been dumped by email, text message, or Facebook can attest, sometimes it is better to talk to someone by phone or meet with them in person, to deliver bad news. Even though we use email for everything, email is not always the best way to communicate bad news.

Why? Because at least a small part of being a good lawyer is being a good person. And a big part of being a good person, especially in a survival situation, is being sensitive to the feelings of others. Depending on the circumstances, delivering bad news in an email is not the most sensitive way to go. So you should only use email to deliver bad news when it feels appropriate. Before you write an "I have bad news" email, make sure that you should not be making a bad news phone call or having a bad news meeting instead.

The appropriate method for giving someone bad news depends on three factors: 1) the relationship you have with the recipient, 2) the nature of the bad news you are delivering, and 3) the impact the bad news is likely to have on you, the recipient, and the case.

## a. The Relationship

Be intuitive. Use what you know about your relationship with the recipient to figure out whether an "I have bad news" email would be a good idea. Do you always communicate with this person by email? Is this person traveling so he or she is not likely to get your phone call or voicemail? If you had good news to deliver, would you more likely send it by email or call the person to talk about it?

When I worked as a litigator for high-tech companies, many of the in-house attorneys did everything by email. I never spoke to them on the phone. In contrast, one of the partners I worked with was so overwhelmed by the hundreds of emails he received every day that if I had something important to tell him, he expected me to call or come by his office. You want to use your previous interactions with the recipient to determine whether an "I have bad news email" is the right choice.

## b. The Nature of the Bad News

Next, consider the kind of bad news you are delivering. Is it very serious? Is it your fault? Would an email give you an opportunity to carefully couch and explain the bad news? Is the bad news something you would rather not put in writing?

I would often communicate judicial orders to my clients by email, especially when it was an order deciding a non-dispositive motion. For example, if the court denied a motion to compel that we had filed, I would send that to my client by email with an explanation of the court's decision. The denial of a motion to compel is bad news, but it is not so important, or such bad news, that it warrants a phone call. Indeed, calling my client to talk about it would be unnecessary and make it seem like a bigger deal than it was. By sending the news in an email, I communicated not only what had happened, but that it was not something to be too worried about.

Now, depending on the client, if a court issued a major order granting or denying a dispositive motion or ordering us to do something, I would call my client first, before forwarding the order by email. Calling the client would allow me to do some damage control and give my client some perspective on the bad news.

## c. The Impact of the Bad News

Last, consider the impact that the bad news may have on you, the recipient, and the case. Does the bad news require immediate action? Does the bad news require a change in case strategy? Will the recipient of the bad news need to make a major decision in light of the bad news? Is the recipient likely to have a bunch of questions about what the bad news means? Would it be better if the recipient had some time to think about the bad news? Do you need to do some research to figure out what should happen next?

I once had to pass along a piece of bad news to a client explaining that a strategy we had used in a case had not worked out as we had planned. The court had denied our motion to dismiss, and we were now in a situation where we had to ramp up our discovery efforts on short notice. I decided to convey this news by email, rather than over the phone, because an email allowed me to set out a plan for getting started with discovery. The bad news in the email was tempered by my detailed description of possible next steps. Thus, you always want to think about whether the impact of the bad news makes it more appropriate for email or some other method of communication before you send an "I have bad news" email.

## 2. First Aid

OK. You have decided that a bad news email is your best option. Now you have to write it in a way that does not make you sound like a jerk.

Being aware of your tone is critical in any email, but especially in a bad news email. Unfortunately, tone is the hardest thing to get across. That is why emoticons were invented.[1] A little smiley face helps to convey all the tone that gets lost with just words and punctuation. But emoticons are not an option here. Seriously. Let me say that again. Emoticons are never an option in any kind of professional email.

The tone of an email is informed by so many little things — a word choice here, a formatting choice there — that it can be hard to diagnose what gives an email a certain tone. But there are two concrete ways that you can control the tone of a bad news email: 1) by using pronouns carefully, and 2) by avoiding legalese.

### a. Choose Your Pronouns Carefully

In an "I have bad news" email, you want to be really thoughtful about how you use pronouns like "I," "you," "we," "us," and "they." Depending on the pronouns you choose, an email can either convey that "we are all in this together" or "you are stranded by your-

---

1. If you have ever sent or received an email, I assume you know this, but "emoticon" is just a fancy word for a smiley face, a sad face, or basically any kind of face created through combinations of keyboard characters. If you have never sent or received an email, I imagine that you are a time traveler here from the distant past (or at least the 1980s). If so, welcome!

self on an iceberg of bad news." For example, what do the pronouns in this email communicate to your client?

> I received a notification earlier today of a negative re-sult in your case. Your motion for reconsideration was denied. You will need to pay Plaintiff $1 million by the end of this week.

Using "you" repeatedly in a bad news email, as this one does, con-veys to the client that he or she is totally alone in the bad news. Tech-nically, that may be true. You probably are not going to chip in on that $1 million payment. Nevertheless, the subtle use of pronouns can change the tone of an email dramatically. From both a client relations and a human sensitivity standpoint, that is a good idea.

The use of "I" and "you" in the previous example sets up a sharp distinction between the lawyer and the client. Where you can do so while still being accurate, using "we" and "our" would smooth over some of the harshness in the message. For example, you could write as follows:

> We received a notification earlier today of a negative re-sult in the case. Our motion for reconsideration was denied.

Substantively, the email has not changed. But using "we" instead of "I" and "our" instead of "your" makes the email sound less harsh and more sympathetic to the recipient.[2]

For the last sentence, you want to see whether there is a way to massage *You will need to pay Plaintiff $1 million by the end of this week*. Rewriting the sentence to avoid using "you" helps to make

---

2. From a malpractice point of view, you want to be careful about using pronouns in such a way that you take responsibility for something that you did not do. Thus, you would not want to say, "when we robbed the bank"; unless, I guess, you did rob the bank with your client. If you and your client are robbing banks together, you probably have bigger prob-lems than the use of pronouns in your professional correspondence. Aside from criminal behavior, you do not want to use "we" to take responsibil-ity for strategic choices made by the client, which could later give rise to a malpractice claim against you.

this sentence more palatable. Losing a case and having to pay $1 million is bad enough; you do not want to rub it in through the haphazard use of pronouns. In this case, "we" are not going to pay the $1 million, so it would not be accurate to say so. But you can add a "we" to the sentence in another way to reframe how you present the payment issue. For example, you could rewrite this sentence as follows:

> We need to discuss the payment to Plaintiff of $1 million by the end of this week.

This sentence begins with "we" by describing what you and the client will do together. Then, this revision uses passive voice and a nominalization to avoid having to use the pronoun "you." A sentence in passive voice makes the object into the subject of the sentence. Here, the part of the sentence about paying Plaintiff $1 million has been phrased passively. The sentence does not expressly state who is going to pay Plaintiff. It also makes the verb "to pay" into the nominalization "the payment," which sounds less frightening.

Now, you might be concerned that the revised version of this sentence is longer than the original. You are absolutely right. Here, two additional words make the sentence more sympathetic and improve the tone of the email. But passive voice and nominalizations are often disfavored in legal writing because they make sentences longer and wordier.[3] In one situation, you may decide that a little artfulness is worth the extra words to avoid distressing your client. In a different situation, you may decide that frankness and a splash of cold water is more important. Survival is about making the right choice for your particular situation.

### b.  Avoid Legalese

You probably know that legalese, formalities, and jargon are disfavored in legal writing. But legalese can be hard to resist in professional correspondence. You should avoid legalese because you do

---

3. Indeed, passive voice and nominalizations are discouraged in Chapter I, Section C, Part 2 of this very book!

not want to seem like a different person in writing than you are in person. When delivering bad news, your goal is effective communication, not showing off your vocabulary. When you are writing an "I have bad news" email, you should put on your most normal-person hat and use language that a real person can understand.

A bad news email that is full of unnecessary jargon will just scare and frustrate the recipient. Unless causing fright and frustration is the goal of your email, using legalese is going to impede, rather than advance, your message. For example, you could write as follows:

> At the conclusion of the oral argument on the motion for reconsideration, the court adjourned and took the matter under advisement.

You could, however, write this same message using simpler language.

> The court did not rule on the motion at the hearing. We will have to wait for the court's decision.

These messages say the same thing, but the first example uses legal jargon and has an aloof tone that may alienate the recipient. In contrast, the second example describes what happened in accessible, plain English.

## 3. Recovery

Optimism is a big part of survival. To get through being lost in the woods, adrift at sea, or ambushed by monkeys you need to be able to look on the bright side. The same is true when you are writing an "I have bad news" email. In your email, you want to include any good news or upside that you can. You also want to describe any next steps, so the recipient understands what the future will look like in light of the bad news that you just delivered. You want the recipient of your email to know that you are going to do everything you can to control the fallout from the bad news. As a legal writing survivalist, keeping your eyes forward is the best policy. If your bad news email can convey an optimistic outlook, it will help the recipient and it will make you look like a real mensch.[4]

If there really is no good news or upside, then at least end the email with something that offers reassurance and comfort. I recommend a version of "please call me directly at any time to discuss." That way the recipient at least knows that he or she can reach out to you upon receiving the bad news. And if you do not get a call or response within a reasonable time after sending your bad news email, follow up. Not hearing from someone after sending bad news can be a sign that he or she is in denial or that your bad news did not come through. Whatever it is, you want to lob in a friendly phone call to make sure that the recipient has not given up hope.

# B. The "I Was Wrong" Email

Many of us stubborn, know-it-all types who choose to be lawyers think that being wrong is the worst thing that can happen to a person. We would rather get eaten by a bear, stung by a wasp, or buried in an avalanche under one hundred feet of snow than admit that we got something wrong. But here is the truth: At some point in your legal career, you are going to be wrong.

I know a guy[5] who, like so many lawyers, does not like to be wrong. He really hates it. When he was a kid he dreamed of being a baseball player. But he did not imagine being a normal baseball player. Oh no. He imagined himself as a baseball player who only hit home runs. Do you understand how crazy this is? He wanted to be a baseball player who hit a home run *every single time* he came to the plate.

As a lawyer, you cannot hit a home run every time. Being a lawyer does not work that way. In just one day as a lawyer you do

---

4. Obviously, you do not want to go so overboard with your optimism that you promise things that you cannot deliver. Your optimism should be tempered by pragmatism. It may be tempting to end every bad news email with a promise to buy the recipient a puppy, but that is not a good idea.

5. In the interest of full disclosure, I am actually married to this guy.

so many hard things and make so many tough calls; it is impossible for them all to be home runs. Statistically,[6] I think a baseball player who only hits home runs is more likely than a lawyer who never gets anything wrong.

Sometimes when you are wrong, you will have to send an email telling someone. This could be another associate, a senior attorney, or your client. I know you are thinking that in this situation it might be better to take a cyanide pill, like a spy who has been captured by the enemy. Please do not do that. You will soon see that you can write an "I was wrong" email and survive.[7]

Most "I was wrong" emails have three goals: 1) to inform others who need to know about your "I was wrong" situation, 2) to offer solutions and next steps in light of the situation, and 3) to protect yourself. When lawyers make mistakes there are consequences. But a carefully written "I was wrong" email will give you some control over how the mistake will be understood by the people who matter.

These are the four steps to surviving an "I was wrong" email: 1) remain calm, 2) investigate and plan, 3) adapt, and 4) keep going.

## 1. Remain Calm

Maintaining perspective is critical to weathering any survival situation, including an "I was wrong" email. As a person who hates to be wrong, realizing that you were wrong can feel like a matter of life or death. It is not. You will be fine. Your career is more than this one mistake. You have done so many good things, and you will do so many more good things. Your job now is to keep it together so that you can resolve the situation and move on with your life.

---

6. There are no statistics for this, although I am sure that the Society for American Baseball Research ("SABR") is working on it.

7. This section is for the kind of small, correctable errors that happen relatively often in the practice of a busy attorney. If something has gone majorly wrong, on the scale of real malpractice, this section is not what you need.

In fact, in any "I was wrong" situation, the person who usually makes it terrible is you. If instead of losing your marbles, you remain calm and maintain your perspective, you will see that everything will work out. Indeed, the situation will work out much better if you do not panic, freak out, or break things. Instead, try to remain calm by knowing that you will survive.

Also, take a moment to think about the other people affected by your "I was wrong" situation. Depending on what happened, this may not be all about you. If you were wrong about something that risks your client's case or your firm's reputation, then you need to keep it together so that you can fix the situation for the other people involved. If you were entrusted with enough responsibility to make a mistake that impacts other people, you owe it to them to do your best to put the pieces back together.

So before you send this "I was wrong" email, try to find a healthy perspective. Remind yourself of something good you have done. Remind yourself of a moment when you felt confident and capable. Remind yourself that things could totally be worse. Take a deep breath.

## 2. Investigate and Plan

Now that you are feeling calm, try to figure out what actually went wrong and what you are going to do about it. As a lawyer and a survivor, if you have the mindset that everything you do is perfect, you are wrong. And if you have the mindset that you cannot get anything right, you are also wrong. The truth is in the middle.

Before you send an "I was wrong" email, you want to be absolutely sure that you understand why you were wrong. The investigation stage is critical to your survival for two reasons: 1) you do not want to say you were wrong if you were not wrong, and 2) you probably are not going to be able to get this situation turned around if you do not understand how you got this thing wrong in the first place.

You need to be able to take responsibility for what you do as an attorney. But you do not want to take responsibility for something that is not your fault.[8] When you think you may have gotten something wrong, take a clear-eyed look at the situation. Own what is yours and attribute the rest where it belongs. Be honest. Do not "pass the buck" or "play the blame game." Just be straight about what happened.

The following five steps will help you to investigate and plan when you have gotten something wrong: 1) assess what happened accurately, 2) choose your method of communication wisely, 3) describe what happened impassively, 4) diagnose what happened sharply, and 5) give yourself a pep talk.

## a. Assess Accurately

Imagine that you calendared the due date for interrogatory responses, but you did not count a holiday that should have been counted. The responses are now due tomorrow when everyone on the team thinks they are due in two days.[9]

Your first step is to make sure that you were wrong. You need to confirm that you originally calendared the wrong date. You should look up the rule on how to calculate deadlines and recalculate the due date. If possible, you should also ask someone else how he or she would calculate the due date. Choose an approachable person who is happy to help you and is not going to be judgmental. After this step, you will understand exactly what you got wrong.

## b. Choose Your Method of Communication Wisely

If you were wrong, your second step is to decide whether this "I was wrong" situation is something that you want to handle via

---

8. If for some crazy reason you *are* going to take responsibility for something that is not your fault, you want to do it knowingly. In literature, characters often do this in a valiant, but misguided attempt to protect someone they love. This just does not have much applicability to the world of modern American legal practice. I liked many of my law firm colleagues very much, but never once did my noble heart drive me to take the blame for something I did not do.

9. This is merely an example. Please do not use anything in this section as an authority on how to calculate a due date for anything.

email. When you are uncomfortable, email can be easier than picking up the phone or talking face-to-face. But remember, emails are forever. Any email you send can theoretically get saved or forwarded or can even reappear during your annual performance review. So before you write the "I was wrong" email, think hard about whether you would be better off using another method of communication.

### c. Describe Impassively

If you decide that an email is the way to go, your third step is to describe what is wrong in the most straightforward, non-hysterical way possible. Try doing this in one simple sentence. Right now, you are just doing this for yourself. You do not need to show it to anyone. Here is a good example:

> The due date for the interrogatory responses is tomorrow, Wednesday, September 17, not two days from now as I originally calculated.

Here is a bad example:

> In the worst calendaring mistake anyone has ever made in the history of American law, I failed to correctly calculate the due date for the interrogatory responses, and we now have to get them ready by tomorrow(!!!) and not Thursday as I originally thought.

You want the most reasonable part of you to write this description. You want to be impassive and describe what is wrong without any melodrama. You want to be accurate, but you do not want to make the situation any worse than it actually is. You want the description of what you got wrong to be as tight as a SCUBA suit.

### d. Diagnose Sharply

Your fourth step is to figure out why you made the mistake. You want to make sure you understand why you originally calendared a different date. Here again, you want to rely on a very reasonable part of yourself. And you want to diagnose what went wrong as precisely as possible. You did not calendar the wrong date because you are a bad person or a bad lawyer. You did not calendar the wrong date because you can never get anything right. You calendared the wrong date because you made one specific mistake. Describe what actually happened because it will help you to organize your thoughts:

> I just realized that I calendared the wrong date because I did not count the Labor Day holiday when counting the thirty days we have to respond to the interrogatories. Under Federal Rule of Civil Procedure 6, any holidays should be counted unless the due date falls on the holiday. I confused the rule and calendared a date that is one day later than the day the responses are actually due.[10]

You will figure out how to incorporate this description into your "I was wrong" email in a moment, but seeing what happened in black and white, without recriminations, should help you start to feel better.

### e. Pep-Talk Time

Your last step is to give yourself a pep talk. Looking at this simple, non-judgmental description of what you got wrong should give you a sense that this situation is going to be OK. It was an honest mistake. The kind anyone could make. It happened because you were tired, confused, distracted, misinformed, or not paying attention. Or it just happened because it happened. You did not do it on purpose. And you will not do it again. Now, you are going to take the steps necessary to fix it.

To be a good lawyer or a good survivor does not mean that you will never make mistakes. Instead, it means that you will work with enthusiasm and creativity to fix the mistakes that are inevitable.

---

10. Again, do not use this to actually calendar due dates in your real-life law practice.

## 3. Adapt

Once you understand what you got wrong and why, you may start to see a way out of the situation. And the sooner you start contemplating a solution to what went wrong, the better you will feel. Few things in lawyering are as satisfying as solving problems. An "I was wrong" situation gives you a great chance to solve a problem.

### a. Audience

Before writing your "I was wrong" email, consider your audience. Use your gut to get a sense of the recipients of your email. Are they patient? Impatient? Pragmatic? Dramatic? Do they focus on solutions? Do they dwell on problems? Any information that you have about the personalities of the recipients of your email will help you craft an "I was wrong" email that does its job of informing others, offering solutions, and protecting you.

### b. Style and Substance

The tone of your "I was wrong" email is important. You should craft your email with your specific audience in mind and follow these general guidelines:

- **Do not over apologize.** A willingness to apologize is a lovely trait for a human being. An apology is the best way to mend hurt feelings. But for work mistakes, an apology is rarely necessary or appropriate because it does not help to fix the problem.[11]
- **Do not lie.** This should be obvious. After getting something wrong, the last thing you want to do is make it worse by lying about it in an email. Remember that the cover up often turns out to be worse than the crime.[12]

---

11. If you feel like you need to apologize in your "I was wrong" email, write an extremely simple and professional apology. Apologies are discussed in more detail in Chapter IV, Section D, Part 2(a).

12. Watergate is probably the most famous example, but there was also the time in first grade when I tried to throw away a math test that I

- **Do not load up your email with justifications.** If there is an understandable reason for what happened, include it. For example, perhaps the rule is ambiguous or you based your conclusion on wrong information that you received from a senior attorney. If you can describe the reason succinctly and in a way that does not make it appear that you are throwing someone under the bus or making excuses, you should do it. Otherwise, it is not worth it. Justifications waste your recipient's time and do not help to correct your "I was wrong" situation.
- **Be concise.** Describe what happened in the most concise way possible. This is the place where you want to wield all of your powers of brevity. The more words and space in your email that you devote to describing what went wrong, the bigger and more terrible it will seem. You want most of your "I was wrong" email to be looking forward. Your recap of what went wrong is only to provide background and context. You are not writing a confession.
- **Be positive about yourself.** If you are a champ for discovering the mistake, make that clear. You want to get any props you can. So if you can give yourself a little credit for discovering you were wrong before the situation went completely awry, include that in your email.
- **Be your own lawyer.** Use neutral words. Describe what happened without commentary, judgment, or assigning blame. For example, rather than writing,

> I failed to calendar the correct date.

It would be better to write,

> The correct date was not calendared.

The second example removes the heavy word "failed" and uses the passive voice to diffuse the judgmental tone of the sentence. When describing something that

---

had failed, and my brother found it and gave it to my mother. That stupid math test haunts me to this day.

you got wrong, passive voice is often your best friend. Passive voice removes the subject from the sentence. When that subject would be you admitting that you got something wrong, the better choice will often be to leave it out.

- **Offer solutions.** The substance of your "I was wrong" email should be about solutions. If possible, offer more than one. Devote most of the email to describing the solutions you have come up with and explaining their pros and cons. By offering solutions, you transform yourself from the person who got everyone into this mess to the world's best problem solver.

### c. *Organization*

After the shortest of pleasantries, begin your email with a sentence or two of background.

> As you know, I have been working on preparing the responses to Plaintiff's interrogatories.

Next, plug in your brief, factual, and non-hysterical description of what you got wrong.

> The due date for the responses is tomorrow, Wednesday, September 17, not two days from today as originally calculated.

Note that this version is slightly different from the original version because it uses passive voice to remove the "I."

Then, consider providing some context for how this happened. You want this to be extremely brief, but accurate. Again, do not lie. And if you can make yourself look good in how you discovered the error, include that for sure.

> Today, as I was double checking all of our discovery deadlines, I realized that I did not count the Labor Day holiday, which is required under Federal Rule of Civil Procedure 6, when counting the thirty days we have to respond to the interrogatories.

Now, offer solutions.

> I suggest that we contact opposing counsel immedi-
> ately and ask for a one-day extension. We recently
> granted Plaintiff's request for an extra week to produce
> documents, so this should not be a problem.

> We could also provide the more limited responses we
> have already prepared, and then supplement our re-
> sponses at a later time.

Last, sound eager to follow through.

> Please let me know if you would like to discuss, or if I
> should go ahead and email opposing counsel about the
> extension.

By describing the mistake plainly and concisely, offering a menu
of solutions, and presenting yourself as a problem solver, your "I
was wrong" email transforms your mistake into a "no harm/no
foul" situation for the recipient.

## 4. Keep Going

You sent the "I was wrong" email and survived. Your job now is
to learn what you can from what happened. You do not want to
make the same mistake twice. So take stock of all the lessons that
came along with your mistake. Then, you need to keep going. If
you are anything like me, you will remember being wrong long
after it has been forgotten in the collective memory of your colleagues. Everyone else just wants to fix the problem and go back to
thinking about what they are going to have for lunch. You should
do the same.

# C.  The "I Need Help" Email

As a lawyer and a survivor, there are times when you are going
to need help. Maybe a project cannot be finished by the deadline.
Maybe an assignment has turned out to be much more compli-

cated than you initially thought. Or maybe you are working on something that requires a high-level strategic decision before you can get started. The problem with asking for help is that you are probably someone who has been rewarded throughout your life for being able to get things done on your own, so asking for help can be hard. But survival for an attorney always requires teamwork. The practice of law is too demanding for you to be a lone wolf for long. You do not want to be the person who would have survived, if you had just been willing to ask for help.

Needing help is not a bad thing, especially when it is preceded by a demonstration of self-reliance. If you really need help, and you have already done everything possible to help yourself, asking for help is not a sign of weakness, laziness, or lack of a can-do spirit. In fact, with the right "I need help" email, you will not only get the help you need, you will also end up looking like a real champ.

 Here are the three simple steps for an effective "I need help" email: 1) make a list, 2) ask for help, and 3) say thank you.

## 1. Make a List

First, figure out what you need. A good way to do this is to write a list. Think of all of the things that would help you and write them down. At this point, you are just spitballing, so do not limit yourself. You are going to whittle down this list before sending the email, but right now you are trying to get a sense of everything you need.

For example, imagine that you were assigned a memo and the senior attorney wanted it by tomorrow. Unfortunately, you had a million emergency projects come up this week on your other cases and you have not even started. In addition, before you can write the memo, you need to get a bunch of production documents copied so that you can rely on them when writing the memo. The paralegal assigned to the case is busy with other projects and says that she does not have time to help you. What would your list look like?

*What I need:*
*1.   More time to write the memo*

2.  *Someone to pull the production documents*
3.  *A vacation*

## 2. The Cry for Help

The most effective "I need help" email is usually the one that gets you the help you need, but makes life as easy as possible for the recipient. You want the person who receives your email to be able to help you without any more inconvenience than absolutely necessary. To do this, you should write an "I need help" email that has two parts: 1) the windup and 2) the pitch. In the windup, you provide context. In the pitch, you ask for the specific help you need.

### a. The Windup

For the windup, your goal is to explain why you need the help you are going to ask for in the pitch. But the windup should not only provide some background, it should also do some marketing. You want to use the windup to build good feelings with the person you are asking for help.

How you do this depends on your relationship with the person you are asking for help. Is the recipient a senior attorney? Is the recipient a person who is junior to you, like a paralegal, legal assistant, or summer intern? Is the recipient another attorney on your same level? You want your request for help to be catered to the relationship you have with the recipient.

**Senior Attorney:** When asking a senior attorney for help, you want to make it clear that you have done everything else possible to find an alternative source for this help. You want the senior attorney to know that you are coming to him or her for help only as a last resort.[13]

In addition, you want to make it clear, if it is true, that you are asking for assistance for some reason that makes you look really good. Your "I need help" email is a great time for public relations. For example, maybe you need help because you have just spotted

---

13. This same concept is addressed at length in Chapter I, Section D.

an issue that no one else working on the case had noticed. Or maybe you need help because you are the only junior attorney staffed on the case and you have been handling the day-to-day work on the case completely on your own. As long as it is subtle and brief, you should try to work a humble brag[14] into your "I need help" email to a senior attorney.

For example, your windup could say something like the following:

> I have been working hard on the memo. Because you have passed my other memos along to the client, I want to be sure that my analysis is thorough and based on a detailed review of all of the relevant documents, some of which have not yet been pulled from the production or reviewed by any other attorney.

This windup is effective because it does a little self-promotion by reminding the senior attorney of your previous good work on the case. It then frames the request for help as an outgrowth of your desire to do a thorough and reliable job.

**Junior Attorney or Staff Person:** When asking someone for help who is junior to you, it is a great idea in the windup to express gratitude to him or her for any assistance you have received in the past. Your "I need help" email should not be the first time that you have thanked this person for helping you,[15] but even if it is, now is a great time to let this person know how much you appreciate the help. By simply expressing gratitude to those who help you, you can be a person whom everyone likes to work with.

---

14. A humble brag is when someone makes a self-aggrandizing statement but couches it in specious humility. In the law firm context, many associates use humble bragging to tell other associates how many zillions of hours they have billed, like this: "I am such a dope. I billed 800 more hours this year than is required for the max bonus," or "I billed 9 million hours and now my bonus is $10,000 more than the maximum for my year. I don't even have the time to spend it!"

15. See Chapter IV, Section C, Part 3 for some additional nagging about the importance of expressing gratitude.

Your windup to a junior person should also acknowledge what you know about his or her current workflow. If you know that the person is busy or that the person has some extra time, you should say so. Being upfront with what you know about this person's availability will help you set the stage for your request for help.

For our example, your windup to a junior person could say the following:

> Thank you so much for your help last week with the document production. You did such a great job getting everything ready in record time. I totally understand that you are swamped right now on this case. If you have a second, I would be happy to talk about how we can prioritize the tasks that are more immediate and maybe put some others on the back burner.

This windup is effective because it states specifically why you are grateful for this person's help. It also explains what you know about this person's availability to establish that you will help this person make time to help you.

**Cohort:** When asking for help from someone on your level, your best bet is usually to appeal to his or her sense of camaraderie. First, you should acknowledge that he or she is probably crazy-busy like you. Doing so puts the two of you in the same boat. Then, you should state that you would be willing to do the same for him or her if the situation were reversed. Many attorneys will appreciate having you owe them one. And you should let your colleague know that you will give him or her credit when discussing the task with the senior attorney.

In our example, your windup could be as follows:

> I know you have been completely slammed lately, but I am in such a pinch today that I don't know what I am going to do. You know you can always ask me for help. I am more than happy to return the favor. I will make sure to mention to [senior attorney] that you offered to help, even though you are really busy.

This windup is effective because it acknowledges your common suffering and offers the promise of help in the future.

## b. The Pitch

In the pitch you ask for the help you need. Try to be as specific as possible. If you are under a deadline, make sure to include that in your email. If you are presenting the recipient with options, present those options as concisely as possible and make it clear which option you believe to be the best. And where you can, limit the amount that the recipient has to do. You want to do anything you can to make it easy for the recipient to help you.

**Senior Attorney**: Your pitch to a senior attorney should ask for enough help that you will not have to send another email asking for more help in the near future. The pitch should also be as accommodating as possible to the senior attorney's schedule and preferences.

For our example, your pitch could look like this:

> If I could have another three days to complete the memo, I know that it would be a much more thorough and useful product. I will make sure to get the memo to you before you leave on Thursday for California, so that you can read it on the plane.

If you are asking a senior attorney for help who is not known for quick responses, you should consider phrasing the pitch as a "silence equals consent" proposition. That means that you should propose the help you need, and then tell the person that you will proceed accordingly, if you do not hear otherwise by a certain time. With this technique, you can save the senior attorney the hassle of dealing with this issue. A major caveat: You only want to use this technique when the consent is for something that you are certain the senior attorney would agree to. Also, you should be sure that you give the senior attorney enough time to see your email before you proceed as though you have his or her consent. Here is an example:

> I am going to ask the paralegal to put off collecting documents for production until the documents I need for the memo have been located and pulled. If you think that this is not the best solution, please let me know by 3

p.m. today. At that time, if I have not heard from you,
I will go ahead and have her switch gears.

**Junior Attorney or Staff Person:** The pitch you send to a junior
person should be realistic in what you are asking for. You do not want
to underestimate the task that you are asking him or her to do. You
also want to be specific in defining the help you need and when
you need it.

Your pitch could read as follows:

> I need you to pull and copy all of the documents from
> the last production that relate to sales and marketing
> by the end of the day. I think it should be about 500
> pages. You should prioritize this ahead of any of your
> other projects.

**Cohort:** The pitch that you send to your cohort needs to be sensitive to tone. Because you are asking someone on your level for
assistance, you want to avoid sounding bossy. You also want to be
realistic about the scope of the task and any deadlines.

In our example, your pitch to your cohort could be as follows:

> I need help reviewing about 500 pages of sales and mar-
> keting documents by the end of the day. I was hoping
> that I could review half of the documents and you would
> review the other half. Some of the documents are pretty
> dense financials. I think it is going to take between five
> and eight hours to do it.

### c. Organization

Now, while not analogous in baseball terms, sometimes the
windup comes after the pitch. When you start with the windup,
the recipient is primed for the pitch. But when you start with the
pitch, you get right to the point. The best organizational structure
for your email will depend on the recipient and the circumstances
of your request.

Think about whether the recipient will be expecting your request, or whether it will come as a surprise. If the recipient expects

it, jump in with the pitch and then explain the context. If the recipient will be surprised, the windup should come first to get the recipient ready to hear the pitch.

Here is our sample "I need help" email to a senior attorney organized with the windup first:

> Dear [name of senior attorney],
>
> I have been working hard on the memo you asked me to prepare. Because you have passed my other memos directly along to the client, I want to be sure that my analysis is thorough and based on a detailed review of all of the relevant documents, some of which have not yet been pulled from the production or reviewed by any other attorney.
>
> If I could have another three days to complete the memo, I know that it would be a much more thorough and useful product. I will make sure to get the memo to you before you leave on Thursday for California, so that you can read it on the plane.
>
> Thank you.

Here is our sample "I need help" email organized with the pitch first:

> Dear [name of senior attorney],
>
> I am hoping that I could have another three days to complete the memo that you asked me to prepare. With a little extra time, I know that it will be a much more thorough and useful product. I can make sure to get the memo to you before you leave on Thursday for California, so that you can read it on the plane.
>
> I have been working hard on the memo, but because you have passed my other memos directly along to the client, I want to be sure that my analysis is thorough

and based on a detailed review of all of the relevant documents, some of which have not yet been pulled from
the production or reviewed by any other attorney.

Thank you.

## 3. Say Thank You

My hope is that your "I need help" email resulted in so much
help that you can hardly believe it. Or maybe, your "I need help"
email resulted in just a teeny, tiny, little bit of help—enough to
help you survive. Either way, you now have a great opportunity to
express some gratitude.

It may seem ridiculous to imagine a law office as a hotbed of
gratitude. We lawyers are not necessarily in the habit of thanking
others for their good work. Instead, we demand that everyone we
work with, especially support staff and junior attorneys, do the
maximum possible and do it perfectly. We may fear that thanking
someone for helping us would send the wrong message. Maybe it
would let that person think that the bar for good work is set at a lower
level. Maybe it would imply that the person is not expected to be
so helpful or do such a good job. Maybe if we went around thanking people all the time, we would look naïve and soft. We do not
thank the sun for rising or thank our cars for driving, so why should
we thank people for doing what they are being paid to do?

Such fears are silly. When someone helps you out, you should
be grateful and express that gratitude with sincerity. Being the
lawyer who is willing to say "thank you" will do astounding things
for you as a person and for your career. It will make your life better. I do not want to get all "Oprah" on you about gratitude, but I
highly recommend being grateful whenever you get the chance.
You should thank the person who responded to your "I need help"
email, and you should also thank anyone that person recruited to
help you. While you are at it, you should thank anyone else you
can think of. Your gratitude might be the first sincere thanks your
colleagues have received in days, months, or years. It will make
them feel great. And you too.

# D. The "I Did Not Mean To Send That Earlier Email" Email

What follows may seem obvious, and I am sure you think that you do not need to hear it, but the best way to avoid having to send an "I did not mean to send that earlier email" email is to not send that earlier email. You do not have to send that "reply all" that you actually meant for just one person. You do not have to accidentally send that sarcastic retort to the very person you are mocking. You do not have to unintentionally forward your mother's embarrassing email to the entire office. How much human suffering could be avoided if we all just waited one more second before we pressed send? Too much to measure. Pressing send judiciously will save you much unhappiness in your life as a lawyer.

This is one survival situation that you can completely avoid. It is less like being stranded on a desert island and more like shooting yourself in the foot. The easiest way to avoid sending a regrettable email is to not send emails higgledy-piggledy and willy-nilly from your phone or while distracted by other things. I know. You love your phone. I love mine too. So much. But I also blame it for most of the unfortunate emailing that I have done in my life.

The rest of the unfortunate emailing that I have done in my life can be blamed on sending emails that should never have been sent in the first place. There are things you should not put in writing. As much as possible, try to express jokes and frustrations in person or over the phone, not through email. Emails do a terrible job of accurately conveying tone or nuanced emotions. And it is so easy for them to fall into the wrong inbox.

When you send the email that you did not mean to send, and then you have to send the "I did not mean to send that earlier email" email, here are three tips for the best way to do it: 1) soothe yourself, 2) respond appropriately, and 3) adopt a closer's mentality so you can learn and move on.

## 1. Self-Soothe

When you have sent an email that you did not mean to send, do not act rashly. It is probably best to deal with the situation expeditiously, but not while you are freaking out. So often, we do one dopey thing and then make it worse by trying to fix it when we are still spinning in circles.

This is a good time to employ the survival mechanism of self-soothing. As a lawyer, you need to have a way to stop yourself from going completely bonkers. What works best for me is to have a simple affirmation written on a sticky note that is on my computer monitor. When I start to lose it, I look at this note and feel better. My note says, "Everything is working out." Your note can say anything that calms you down, like "Nothing lasts," "I am good," "Just breathe," or "Remember chocolate-chip cookies." This note does not have to do anything but make you feel a little better. Write something comforting and read it a bunch of times.

## 2. Respond

Your next step is to perform some damage control.[16] Your "I did not mean to send that earlier email" email usually should be a mixture of apology and strategy.

### a. Apologize

Apologizing is probably the one thing that is harder for lawyers than gratitude.[17] Many lawyers resist apologizing for their mistakes.

---

16. Depending on your email system, consider the option of recalling the message. In most situations, however, I would vote against using it. You know that those recall messages often make the situation worse. A recall message alerts everyone to the message that you did not mean to send, and if they already read the original message, they can still read it! What is the point? My suggestion is to only use the recall feature if you are certain that the recipient will not have opened the message. And even then, I probably still would not use it.

17. Although, dancing is right up there too. You would not believe the awkward dancing that I have witnessed at law firm holiday parties.

They believe the fallacy that apologizing is a sign of weakness. In fact, apologizing is good for you. It shows others that you are a human being. And it will help you survive.

If you sent an email that you did not mean to send and hurt the feelings of the recipient, then apologizing is probably the way to go. Apologizing is not necessary for work mistakes, but it is the best thing we have when it comes to human mistakes. Being snarky or making a mean joke is not the worst thing in the world, but refusing to acknowledge it and apologize for it can be. Practicing law is not always kittens and sunshine, but you do not have to be a jerk. Whenever possible in the practice of law, we want to be human beings first.

When an apology is appropriate, think about whether it would be better to apologize in person or over the phone. Getting the tone right for a written apology can be really difficult.

If you do decide to write your apology, focus on apologizing plainly. If you can, apologize for what you wrote that was hurtful, not for something just to the side of it. I had this friend who was always willing to apologize, but she never apologized for the right thing. If she was late to pick me up, instead of apologizing for being late, she would apologize that there was so much traffic where we lived. This kind of apology does not cut it. Be an apologizer, not an apologist.

If an explanation will make your original email and your apology make more sense, include it, but make it brief. If you have accidentally sent someone a mean email, he or she probably does not want to hear a long explanation about why it was not really your fault. But if you can provide a little context that makes the unintentional email seem not so bad, go ahead.

For example, when I was a litigator I worked for a partner who would often give confusing instructions. One time, he emailed another junior attorney and asked her to perform a task. She forwarded the email to me and asked if I understood what he wanted her to do. I was very busy and this attorney had been asking me for help on many of her projects. I felt that she needed to deal with this partner directly. I wrote back, "Not really, but that's because I never understand what he wants. Who does?" I then somehow accidentally included him on the response. Ugh.

As soon as I realized what I had done, I immediately sent another message in which I apologized to him. I told him that I was sorry about what I wrote. I then briefly explained that I was often confused by his instructions—which he knew—but that I was also feeling pinched by being so busy and having to do so much hand-holding of this other attorney. Although this partner could be prickly, he graciously accepted my apology. He also told me that he knew his instructions could be confusing, and that I should be comfortable asking him to clarify. This is as close to a free pass as I could hope for after accidentally sending a glib, critical email about my boss directly to his inbox.

A simple, straightforward apology is an easy fix for many regrettable emails. If your email hurt someone's feelings or was unkind, you just have to be brave enough to apologize.

### b. Strategize

If the email that you did not mean to send was something that will impact your client's case, rather than cause hurt feelings, a simple apology is probably not sufficient. Instead, you need to make a more strategic decision: one that protects you and your client. Malpractice hangs over every practitioner, so you need to be aware of the potential consequences of your unintended email before you decide how to handle it.

In this situation, you need to think through three questions before deciding how to react:

- What needs to be corrected?
- What needs to be massaged?
- What are the real consequences?

Think about corrections first. An email can last forever, so if you wrote something in your unintended email that is wrong, you probably want to correct it. It is rarely in your best interest to have an incorrect email that you wrote floating out in the world uncorrected, even though sending a correction sounds about as appealing as eating nothing but canned peaches for the rest of your life.[18] Try to make the correction without too much editorializing. Do not heap contempt upon yourself while making the correction. Instead, be straightforward and matter of fact.[19]

For example, imagine that your client emails to ask you what day some interrogatory responses are due. You respond quickly from your phone while you are at lunch that they are due in two weeks, but when you get back to the office you see that they are actually due in just a few days. In that situation, you would need to send an email correction to notify your client in writing of the correct date. Although it may make you feel uncomfortable to put in writing that your original email was incorrect, you want to have written proof that you corrected the date. Your correction email should be short and to the point, like this:

> The email that I sent earlier today provided the incorrect due date for the interrogatory responses. They are due Tuesday, November 13, not Tuesday, November 27. Please let me know if you have any questions.

Next, consider anything that you would want to massage, not because it was incorrect, but because it was impolite or impolitic. Your effort to smooth things over may come in the form of an apology, or you may need to say something that is only "apology-esque." Massaging addresses the human side of sending an email that you did not mean to send. It attempts to heal bruised egos or broken connections.

For example, imagine that you sent an email that criticized a conclusion reached by another attorney on your team, but later you discovered that the other attorney's conclusion was correct. You would not need to apologize for being incorrect,[20] but you

---

18. Although, if you plan on surviving any kind of post-apocalyptic scenario, you should start getting used to this idea.

19. Please also see Chapter IV, Section B about sending an "I was wrong" email.

20. If you were rude in how you expressed your criticism, you should apologize. But I would hope that you would not send a rude email in the first place.

would want to acknowledge that the other attorney had it right. Your email should massage the situation by noting that your criticism was unwarranted and by giving credit to the other attorney for reaching the correct conclusion. Your massaging email should say something like the following:

> My previous conclusion was incorrect. [Colleague] was absolutely right and deserves credit for figuring out this complicated issue so quickly. Great work.

Last, think about whether there will be any consequences for you or your client for having sent the email that you did not mean to send. For example, there are numerous examples of attorneys accidentally sending internal strategy emails to opposing counsel. If something like this happens, you want to make a plan about how to handle it. Once you have your plan, you may need to communicate it to your client. You should be delicate in how you describe what happened, and how you plan to fix it. But do not be misleading. You do not have to tell your client, "I did a really dumb thing, and now we have to make it right," but you also should not say, "Due to circumstances completely out of my control, we are now going to make a few changes to our litigation plan." You want to both take responsibility and focus on solving any problems created by the email that you did not mean to send.

## 3. The Closer's Mentality

In any survival situation there are going to be setbacks. Your food might get eaten by raccoons. Your raft might spring a leak. Your socks might get wet. Or you might send an email that you did not mean to send.

When you have a setback, whether it was your fault or not, you have to cultivate a "closer's mentality." In baseball, the closer is the guy who finishes the game to preserve the lead. There is a lot of pressure on a closer. If the closer messes up and the team loses because he blew the lead, he gets all of the blame. But game after game, the closer is expected to do his job. When asked to close a game, a closer cannot sulk about what happened the night before when he gave up a walk-off grand slam. Oh no. The closer has to learn from his mistake, and then give himself a clean slate to pursue his next "save." People who have the closer's mentality learn (or just know) how to immediately put their mistakes behind them. To survive an email that you did not mean to send, you have to cultivate a closer's mentality. Continuing to beat yourself up because the email you sent was dumb, careless, or avoidable does not help you. And pretending it never happened does not help you either. You have to clean it up the best you can, make the necessary adjustments and amends, and move on.

# Chapter V

# Survival Tool Belt: Tips, Tricks, Checklists, and FAQs

This Chapter provides quick reference guides on research, grammar, punctuation, citation, readability, proofreading, and style. These topics are often the key to surviving a legal document. Think of them as your survival tool belt.

## A. Research

Effective research requires organization, creativity, and grit. Here is a checklist to help you make sure your research gets the job done:

- ❏ I verified my understanding of the general area of law using secondary sources.
- ❏ I used my understanding of the hierarchy of authority to correctly identify and search the appropriate sources and jurisdictions.
- ❏ I considered whether authorities were mandatory or persuasive.
- ❏ I read the cases carefully and identified their outcomes, procedural postures, and why they are relevant to my case.
- ❏ I used search terms that varied in their breadth and depth so that my research encompassed all relevant results.
- ❏ I used good results to find additional results by looking at the authorities that cite and are cited in my good results.

❑  I knew that I had completed my research when I re-
    peatedly found the same results that I had already found.
❑  I validated all of the sources that I relied upon to en-
    sure that they are still good law.
❑  I organized my research results in a physical or elec-
    tronic folder so that I can come back to them later and
    understand them, if necessary.
❑  I updated my research results regularly to account for
    any recent changes in the law.

# B. Grammar

An astounding array of grammatical errors can appear in legal
documents. But the list below contains the five errors that I have
noticed most often both as a lawyer and a legal writing professor.

## 1. Pronoun Agreement

When you use a pronoun to refer to a singular noun, you need
to use "he," "she," or "it," not "they." This is true even if you do not
know the gender of the noun you are referring to.

- CORRECT: I heard that a rhinoceros attacked one of
  the plane crash survivors. I hope he or she is OK.
- INCORRECT: I heard that a rhinoceros attacked one
  of the plane crash survivors. I hope they are OK.

Similarly, treat a single court, company, or organization as a
singular noun and use the pronoun "it," not "they."

- CORRECT: The court banned zombies from the courtroom. It ordered all of the living dead to leave.
- INCORRECT: The court banned zombies from the
  courtroom. They ordered all of the living dead to leave.

## 2. Its v. It's

Make "it" possessive by using "its." There is no apostrophe; just like there is no apostrophe in "his." "It's" is a contraction meaning "it is." We rarely use contractions in legal writing because they are too informal, so you are not going to need "it's" in your legal documents.

- CORRECT: The doomsday preparedness organization held <u>its</u> annual meeting in Zanesville, Ohio.
- INCORRECT: The doomsday preparedness organization held <u>it's</u> annual meeting in Zanesville, Ohio.
- ALSO INCORRECT: The doomsday preparedness organization held <u>their</u> annual meeting in Zanesville, Ohio.
- CORRECT: <u>It is</u> a shame that a pack of feral cats ate the last of our food.
- CORRECT, BUT DISFAVORED IN LEGAL WRITING: <u>It's</u> a shame that a pack of feral cats ate the last of our food.
- INCORRECT: <u>Its</u> a shame that a pack of feral cats ate the last of our food.

## 3. Because v. Since

When you mean "because," you should use the word "because." You should only use the word "since" when you are referring to the passage of time.

- CORRECT: <u>Because</u> this nuclear apocalypse is your fault, you better be willing to carry the heavier backpack.
- INCORRECT: <u>Since</u> this nuclear apocalypse is your fault, you better be willing to carry the heavier backpack.
- CORRECT: <u>Since</u> you started this nuclear apocalypse last Wednesday, you have been a real jerk.

## 4. Compound Subject-Verb Agreement

When you have a compound subject separated with "or," the verb should agree with the subject closest to the verb.

- CORRECT: Either the Yeti <u>or the werewolves were</u> responsible for destroying our camp.
- CORRECT, BUT SOUNDS WEIRD: Either the werewolves <u>or the Yeti was</u> responsible for destroying our camp.
- MAY SOUND BETTER, BUT INCORRECT: Either the werewolves <u>or the Yeti were</u> responsible for destroying our camp.

Note: As you can see in the second example, sometimes this rule makes your sentence sound weird, even if it is grammatically correct. This is a sign that you should rewrite the sentence. Lawyers do not get any points for writing something that is technically correct, but sounds terrible.

## 5. Modifier Placement

When you use a modifier, like "only," put it right next to the thing it modifies.

- CORRECT: The survivors <u>liked only chunky peanut butter</u>.
- INCORRECT (UNLESS YOUR POINT IS THAT THE SURVIVORS DID NOT LOVE OR FEEL ANY OTHER EMOTIONS ABOUT CHUNKY PEANUT BUTTER): The survivors <u>only liked chunky peanut butter</u>.

# C. Punctuation

There are three punctuation marks that are frequently misused in legal documents. Here are the rules to use them correctly.

## 1. Apostrophes

Oh, apostrophes. Has there ever been a more abused mark of punctuation? We are in an apostrophe crisis. There are missing and unwarranted apostrophes littering our lives. Here are the rules you need to know:

*Use an apostrophe to make something possessive.*

- CORRECT: The <u>farmer's</u> house looked like an appealing place to stay for the night, but it was overrun with vicious robots.
- INCORRECT: The <u>farmers</u> house looked like an appealing place to stay for the night, but it was overrun with vicious robots.

*Never use an apostrophe to make something plural.*

- CORRECT: My <u>socks</u> are wet, and I have lost feeling in my big toe.
- INCORRECT: My <u>sock's</u> are wet, and I have lost feeling in my big toe.

*Make a word plural before you make it possessive.*

- CORRECT: The three zombie <u>viruses'</u> symptoms have the same symptoms: glowing red eyeballs and a taste for human flesh.
- INCORRECT: The three zombie <u>virus's</u> have the same symptoms: glowing red eyeballs and a taste for human flesh.

*When you have a proper name that ends in s, you can either 1) add an apostrophe, or 2) add an apostrophe s. Pick one approach and be consistent. I prefer to add an apostrophe s.*

- CORRECT: I am so glad that we grabbed the keys to Mr. Jones's motorcycle before the aliens attacked.
- CORRECT: I am so glad that we grabbed the keys to Mr. Jones' motorcycle before the aliens attacked.

## 2. Quotation Marks

Quotation marks are usually fine on their own, but things seem to get crazy when quotation marks meet another punctuation mark. The rules, however, are so simple that you should be able to master this immediately.

*Periods and commas go inside quotation marks. Always. Always. Always. Unless you are British.*

This seems weird because if the quotation marks set off only part of the text of the sentence, it feels like cheating to sneak a period or comma inside the quotation marks. But that is what you do.

- CORRECT: The survivor said to the hippopotamus, "it is you or me, buddy."
- INCORRECT: The survivor said to the hippopotamus, "it is you or me, buddy".
- CORRECT: The survivor said to the hippopotamus, "it is you or me, buddy," and then ran as fast as he could in the other direction.
- INCORRECT: The survivor said to the hippopotamus, "it is you or me, buddy", and then ran as fast as he could in the other direction.

*Semicolons and colons go outside quotation marks, unless they are within the quoted language.*

- CORRECT: The survivor said to the hippopotamus, "it is you or me, buddy"; then he ran as fast as he could in the other direction.

- INCORRECT: The survivor said to the hippopotamus, "it is you or me, buddy;" then he ran as fast as he could in the other direction.
- CORRECT: The survivor had only three "friends": the sun, the moon, and a coconut she had named Arnold.
- INCORRECT: The survivor had only three "friends:" the sun, the moon, and a coconut she had named Arnold.
- CORRECT: The survivor said to Arnold, "I used to love three things: cats, bacon, and sunsets in Key West."

## 3. Semicolons

Use semicolons sparingly. To use them accurately, follow these simple rules.

*The text on each side of the semicolon has to be a complete sentence.*

- CORRECT: The zombies controlled the mountains; the human survivors lived on the beach.
- INCORRECT: The zombies controlled the mountains; not the beach.

*A semicolon should almost never be followed by a coordinating conjunction like "and," "but," or "or." If you are using one of those little words, then use a comma instead. There is one exception: a semicolon can be followed by "and" or "or" when you are using semicolons to separate complex items in a list and you use a coordinating conjunction before the last item.*

- CORRECT: The zombies controlled the mountains; the human survivors lived on the beach.
- INCORRECT: The zombies controlled the mountains; and the human survivors lived on the beach.
- CORRECT UNDER EXCEPTION: The world was divided as follows: the zombies controlled the mountains where the cold air preserved their rotting flesh; the human survivors lived on the beach, which was safe and

provided access to food; and the apes made their home
in the forest, as they had for eons.

# D.  Citation

You surely understand the importance of following the rules of
citation. Proper citation gives your document credibility. It is a se-
cret handshake that tells your reader that you are a member of the
club.

But this book is about survival. And you can survive citation
without following every picayune rule perfectly. In my experience,
after you get out of law school, the real world of law practice does
not have such exacting expectations about citation. In practice,
proper citation comes down to two things: accuracy and consistency. Accuracy means making sure that the information in your
citation is correct, so that the reader can use the citation to find
the exact source, and the exact place in that source, that you are
citing. Consistency means making all citations of the same kind look
the same. Outside of the legal writing classroom and your law
school's law review, if you have accuracy and consistency, perfect
citation format is less important. What you want to avoid is making citation errors that make your reader notice your citations.
And what you really want to avoid is making citation errors that
will make your reader think that you have been sloppy or undis-
ciplined in quoting and citing sources.

The following is a checklist of citation problem areas that lists the
most common citation errors and the most important citation information. If you have limited time to devote to citation, focus on
these things first:

❑   Do you include a citation any time the reader would
      want to know what authority you relied upon for a
      particular assertion?
❑   Do all of your case citations include pinpoint citations
      to the particular page you are referring to, not just the
      first page of the case?

❑ Do you include the year of decision the first time you cite any case?

❑ Do you include the specific section and sub-section any time you cite a statute?

# E. Readability

So much of how a reader perceives a document comes down to its readability. There are four simple things that you can do to make your document easy on the reader.

## 1. Make the First Sentence of Every Paragraph a Clear Topic Sentence

A legal document depends upon topic sentences. Every paragraph in the document should have a first sentence that states your point about the topic of that paragraph. You do not want to write first sentences that are placeholders, which identify the topic of the paragraph, but say nothing substantive about it. Nor do you want the first sentence of any paragraph to be a random assertion somewhat related to the topic of the paragraph. You want the first sentence of every paragraph to be a distillation of the point of that paragraph.

Often, if you take the last sentence of a paragraph and make it the first sentence instead, it will be a great topic sentence. For example, that technique would work well in the preceding paragraph.

## 2. Write Short Sentences and Paragraphs

If you use short sentences and paragraphs liberally, you will make your reader happy. Short sentences are often easier to follow than long sentences, and the white space from the indent of a new paragraph gives the reader a nice break. But you do not have to write only short sentences and paragraphs. Indeed, a document with only short sentences and paragraphs would read like a robot manifesto. You are not a robot.[1]

Try to write sentences that are mostly on the shorter side, with some longer sentences thrown in. Doing so should give you a nice average sentence length between fifteen and twenty words. In addition, try to make your paragraphs longer than one sentence, but shorter than half of a page.

### 3. Use Transition Words to Guide the Reader

To avoid the choppiness that short sentences and paragraphs can cause, use transition words. Some of the best transition words for legal writing are the following conjunctive adverbs:

> *accordingly, also, consequently, further, furthermore, however, indeed, instead, likewise, moreover, nevertheless, otherwise, similarly, then, thereafter, therefore, thus*

When using a transition word, take care to use the one that makes logical and grammatical sense. Also, be careful not to repeat the same transition word multiple times in close proximity.

### 4. Always Have Page Numbers

This is easy, right? Nothing makes a reader who is trying to understand a document crazier than not being able to find a page number. Put page numbers on your documents. Always.

## F. Proofreading

Proofreading is part of the art of writing. If your document is full of correctable mistakes, the reader may think less of your cred-

---

1. If you are a robot, then you must be reading this from a future time when robots have become sentient and entered the practice of law. Welcome to the profession, guys!

ibility and thoughtfulness. Here are some tips to make it easier to proofread efficiently and effectively.

**Proofreading Tip No. 1:** Proofreading is a process.

Proofreading is not something that happens one time in the seconds before you submit your document. Proofreading is a process that occurs throughout the time you write your document. You should be constantly reading and proofreading as you work on your document.

**Proofreading Tip No. 2:** Do not do everything at once.

You cannot proofread your document for every kind of error at the same time. No human being can. Thus, you should proofread for different types of errors at different times. Every proofreading pass through your document should be guided by a specific intention as to the type of error you are looking for. Limiting the focus of each proofreading pass will make the job easier, and it will help you find more errors. You should proofread separately for each of the following issues:

- wordiness
- grammar
- punctuation
- citation
- typos

And while you are doing those passes, you should correct any other errors that you happen to notice. Then, you should do some final proofreading passes where you look for anything odd or off that catches your eye.

**Proofreading Tip No. 3:** Change the font.

Change the font of your document before doing your proofreading. After writing a document, you are so used to what it looks like that when you are proofreading you are not even really reading it any more. You are just remembering it. By changing the font you mix it up in your mind, and you will see things you did not see before. Oh, and make sure to change it back before you print out your document for the final proofreading passes, so that you can make sure that there are no formatting problems.

**Proofreading Tip No. 4:** Print it out.

Print out the pages of your document to proofread it. Although it is faster and more environmentally friendly to proofread your document on the screen, at least one time before you submit your document (and probably more) you should proofread a hard copy. Printing out your document allows you to see whether there is anything strange with the pagination — for example, a heading that is stranded by itself at the bottom of a page — and it provides you with a new view of your document that will help you catch more proofreading mistakes. Afterward, please recycle.

**Proofreading Tip No. 5:** Take one last look.

Once you think you are done because your document could not possibly be any more perfect than it already is (or you have simply run out of time), take a breath, and look over your entire document, including the caption, the signature block, and the headings, one more time. I cannot tell you how often I have caught a serious typo in the last pass through the document. If you give yourself one more chance to catch something, you probably will.

# G. Style

Here are some frequently asked questions and answers about legal writing style.

1. *Should I use party names or designations, like plaintiff, defendant, appellant, appellee, etc., to refer to the parties in my legal documents?*

Names or legally significant terms that reflect the relationship between the parties are almost always better than designations. This is particularly true when you are referring to your own client. But even when referring to the other party, using a name or a legally significant term like "buyer" or "seller" makes the story of the case more interesting for the reader and grounds it in reality.

*2. Can I start sentences with "and"?*

Yes, but only sparingly. You can start sentences with "but" too, but this is a technique that you want to use in a limited way. Starting a sentence with "and" or "but" can help the flow of your writing and allow you to break a long sentence into shorter pieces. But you should use caution with these techniques for the following reasons. First, starting sentences with "and" and "but" may lead you to write sentence fragments. Second, starting sentences with "and" and "but" can become a crutch where you think you are writing short sentences, but you are not offering the reader much relief because every sentence flows right into the next sentence. Last, some readers may view starting sentences with "and" and "but" to be too informal for legal writing.

*3. Can I have paragraphs in my document that are only one sentence?*

Yes, but this technique is another that you want to use sparingly. A paragraph that has only one sentence can disrupt the flow of your document because it stands out abruptly to the reader. Thus, if you give a sentence its own paragraph, it better be a really great sentence.

*4. If you had to identify the one thing that separates a well-written legal document from a document that is not so well written, what would it be?*

Topic sentences. A document in which each paragraph starts with a topic sentence that substantively guides the reader is guaranteed to be easier to read than a document that does not have effective topic sentences.

*5. Would you rather be lost at sea, lost in the woods, or lost in the desert?*

Lost at sea. For sure. A boat might come by at any moment, so there would always be a reason to have hope. Also, there would be no snakes.

# Index